D0055313

The
HAPPY
H☉UR
EFFECT

Also by Kristen K. Brown:

The Best Worst Thing
Beat the Blues

Praise for Kristen K. Brown's The Happy Hour Effect

"Kristen does a great job of identifying the stress areas that are sabotaging your life's energy, and she provides simple and effective steps for demolishing your stress. Kristen's Life Map is a simple, easy-to-use aid that helps you visually transform your life from where it is to where you want it to be. If you were to get only one book this year on ridding your life of stress and finding a much better road map for life, this should be the one!"

—Randy Ganther
speaker and author of *The Little Book for Huge Success*

"Kristen does an excellent job as she uses her experience and expertise to lay out the tools and techniques to help you manage your stress and reach your goals. It's like having your personal coach with you every step of the way. Kristen wants to see you succeed."

—Ornella Grosz, CFEd, personal finance expert, keynote speaker, and author of *Moneylicious: A Financial Clue for Generation Y*

"Looking for a stress-free hour? Spend it with *The Happy Hour Effect: Twelve Secrets to Minimize Stress and Maximize Life*, by Kristen K. Brown. Her casual, friendly writing style makes reading this insightful and practical book feel more like having a chardonnay and flannel pajama conversation with your best girl friend. Filled with novel and imaginative ideas for living a happier, less stressful life, Kristen's advice is bound to educate and motivate you. And her candid portrayal of her own personal challenges will inspire you to leave your whining behind and create your own best life."

—Diane Keyes, home staging expert and award-winning author of
This Sold House: Staging Your Home to Sell in Today's Market

"As a weight loss and wellness expert, I see stress as the number one barrier for people getting their health and weight on track. With Kristen's expertise, readers will be able to change their response to stress to make it a launch pad for a better life instead of dragging them further from their goals. This book is a must-read. It is a key to your energy and success!"

—Jina Schaefer, founder of Discover Health

"The first time we met Kristen (at the Academy Awards), we already knew she was a superstar of energy, vitality, and positivist. She shines! Her work on life balance helps the rest of us learn to do the same."

—Max & Ally Sinclair, Cocopotamus by NYDC Chocolate

"Implementing Kristen's Happy Hour Effect strategies literally changed the way I moved in the world. Thanks to her valuable insights and proven techniques, I am now happier, more balanced, and more successful than ever before! I highly recommend her teachings for anyone who is seeking more out of life than a never-ending to-do list."

—Theresa Rose, national motivational humorist
and award-winning author of *Opening the Kimono:*
A Woman's Intimate Journey Through Life's Biggest Challenges

"Sometimes it takes a tragic event to alert us to a problem. Becoming a widow at age thirty-one with a small child and a demanding job led Kristen K. Brown to discover how stress was affecting her life. She sought to find ways to alleviate this stress. The results are compiled in this book. Along with providing twelve secrets to understanding stress factors, she offers suggestions as to what you can do to reduce stress by changing your thoughts and behavior. Kristen does not deliver foolproof answers, but gives us tools and points us in the right direction so we can take the lifelong journey into a more peaceful life."

—Kathryn Holmes, inspirational speaker and author of
I Stand with Courage: One Woman's Journey to Conquer Paralysis

"*The Happy Hour Effect* was a joy to read and chock full of common-sense strategies to cope with stress. Kristen Brown's *tell it like it is* approach makes it easier to understand stress and the impact it has on us. The Life Map is a framework to recognize areas of stress and strategies to cope with these areas. The Chapter Action Guides are quick reference guides that offer practical, doable solutions. As a human energy consultant, I will definitely recommend *The Happy Hour Effect* to my clients."
—Debra Safyre, human energy consultant and founder of Safyre Catalyst

"*The Happy Hour Effect* by Kristen K. Brown gives you the tools you need to eliminate stress from your life using her flexible plan. From goal setting to a life map, you will learn to simplify your life and attain what makes you happy while eliminating those things that add stress to your life. Everyone needs a copy of this training manual before setting out on the road of life."
—Darlene Arden, certified animal behavior consultant and author of *Rover, Get Off Her Leg!* and *The Complete Cat's Meow*

"Kristen Brown's *The Happy Hour Effect* has completely changed how I look at stress and its effects on my life. Brown's GOALS-oriented approach, reassuring tone, expert background, and personal anecdotes helped me better understand the roots behind my own stress challenges, while her concrete, customizable, step-by-step suggestions provided precisely the guidance I needed to start making positive, stress-busting changes in my life *today*. Here's to *Happy Hour* Cheers!"
—Julia Tagliere, busy mother of three and author of *Widow Woman*

"Is stress preventing you from living the life you desire? Then Kristen Brown has a message for you: it doesn't have to! *The Happy Hour Effect* demystifies stress by providing practical, sound advice for overcoming life's little, and sometimes not-so-little, challenges. Honest, engaging, and humorous, *The Happy Hour Effect* is going on my *must recommend* list."
—Michael Mapes, spiritual coach and motivational speaker

The
HAPPY
H⊙UR
EFFECT

Twelve Secrets
to Minimize Stress
and Maximize Life

KRISTEN K. BROWN
bestselling author of *The Best Worst Thing*

GOODMAN BECK PUBLISHING

Copyright © 2012 by Kristen K. Brown
All rights reserved.

No part of this publication may be reproduced, stored in a retrieval system, or
transmitted, in any form or by any means, electronic, mechanical, photocopying,
recording, or otherwise, without the express written consent of the publisher.

The author and publisher shall have neither liability nor responsibility to any
person or entity with respect to any of the information contained in this book.
The material in this book is provided for educational and informational
purposes only and is not intended as medical advice. The reader assumes
all risk for any injury, loss, or damage caused or alleged to be caused,
directly or indirectly, by using any information described in this book.

GOODMAN BECK PUBLISHING

PO Box 253
Norwood, NJ 07648
goodmanbeck.com

ISBN 978-1-936636-10-5

Library of Congress Control Number: 2012948037

Printed in the United States of America

10 9 8 7 6 5 4 3 2 1

*For Brooke, who reminds me every day to relax, smile,
and make healthy choices so I can have a long, happy,
and low-stress life seeing her grow up! We are nailing it!*

Contents

Introduction

Welcome to The Happy Hour Effect lifestyle! I'm so glad you have taken this step to make your life the very best it can be for you and your loved ones. Every single day we are faced with stress both good and bad. We are bombarded by responsibilities, tasks, to-do lists, and schedules that can suck our energy or energize us depending on how we respond to the demands of everyday life. When we respond positively, stress can motivate us to work harder, faster, and more efficiently to get things done. But when stress goes negative, which is most often the case, it contributes to illness and the leading causes of death. It's so much more than an inconvenience. Stress is killing us—and no one is immune. Even I, *The Queen of Stress Relief*, feel the urge to lash out or crawl into a dark hole sometimes! But over the years, I've discovered the secrets to shifting those feelings of anxiety and frustration into a positive force in my life instead of letting them drag me down.

It wasn't easy. In fact, my journey started after a tragedy in my life. I had just turned thirty-one and was living what I thought was the good life. My husband, Todd, and I had a house, a dog, and a new baby daughter, Brooke. Things weren't perfect. The first year of parenthood is hard, and we definitely had our ups and downs, but we were surviving, and I was determined to get us back to thriving as soon as I got past my sister's wedding weekend. As the maid of honor, I had been wrapped up in wedding details and hadn't made much time for Todd, but as I looked at him from the front of the church the night of the wedding, I made a vow to myself that I would get back on track as soon as we arrived home from that weekend. We were staying at a hotel for the weekend, and on Sunday morning we should have all gotten up and driven the three hours back to our home in Minneapolis. Instead, Todd didn't wake up. He had died of a heart attack in his sleep sometime early that morning. He was thirty years old, tall, skinny, and a former college athlete. He had just had a physical a few months before and been given a clean bill of health. How could something like that happen?

As you can imagine, the stress of that situation was unthinkable. Then, just two weeks later, I was thrust into an extremely challenging situation at the job I had once loved. I got a new supervisor whose behaviors and tactics were very different from mine. I was suddenly not only dealing with the loss of my husband, but the 24/7 demands of a workaholic boss. And then to make matters worse, the economy tanked. I was a widow mom in a job that was sucking me dry, but I stuck in the job because I needed the security during those scary times. The stress ate me alive. I lost twenty pounds. I was sick all the time. I couldn't focus. I also began suffering panic attacks when I had to interact with my boss.

On the surface I kept it together, but underneath I was slowly dying inside, and I knew it. But I was determined not to go on the prescription antidepressants and antianxiety medications that my doctor had recommended. No judgments for those who are on them or have tried them. That just wasn't a choice I wanted to make for myself. I wanted to feel what I was feeling and find a way to manage it naturally and holistically. I knew I had to do it for my daughter. I never wanted her to look back on her childhood and think to herself, "Oh, my mom was so sad," or "My mom was so angry." I only wanted her to look back and remember how fun and happy her mom was—and most importantly, to learn from me that no matter how bad a situation, you *can* find your way out of it with just a little effort and a lot of commitment to change. I may have been left a widow at age thirty-one, but I wasn't going to let that define the rest of our lives.

Over the next couple of years after my husband's death, I began experimenting with stress management techniques, herbs, meditation—anything short of illegal, I tried it. And it is that experimentation that helped me heal and brought me to this point where I now share my expertise to help others overcome their own challenges. I went back to school to get my master's certificate in integral theory (we'll talk about that later in the book) and a holistic health coach certification. And eventually, it all came together into a powerful fusion of life experience, education, and many years in corporate America, which makes me a true expert on stress management and wellness. I provide resources and tools to help others minimize stress and maximize life with my company Happy Hour Effect LLC, including classes, books, study programs, teleseminars, speaking, corporate stress programs, and lots of free articles and tips on Facebook and the company's official website to inspire and motivate people to make small but powerful changes in their lives. And let me tell you, the fulfillment and happiness I get from helping others makes me rich beyond measure—and knowing that I am a role model for my daughter to look up to is a reward in itself.

This book pulls my expertise together into one powerful resource guide. It isn't a book you read once and then put on the shelf. Life is a journey, not a destination. Our lives change every moment just as our needs and wants change every moment. This book and the website that goes along with it provide hundreds of tips and ideas that you can use as your life changes, as it inevitably will. It's not just about stress but about living a healthy and happy life every single day. Keep it on your bedside table or on your desk at work. It is meant to be flexible, easy, and fun so anyone can find the right solution at the right time. And don't be overwhelmed. Start by doing the Life Mapping exercise first. And then think small by choosing one or two ideas to try first. Do *not* try to do more than that when you first get started or you will get overwhelmed by too many changes at once and fail. (More about that later.)

There is no one-size-fits-all solution for stress, and there is no one secret to happiness and health. By using this book, you will learn my secrets, and then it's up to you to have fun with them. Experiment, be open to change, and start trying the suggestions for yourself and your loved ones. It has been a bittersweet journey to get to where I am, but it's led me here where I can arm you with the best secrets for a happier, healthier, and less stressful life. Thank you for joining me as I lead this Stress Less Revolution!

Sincerely,
Kristen Brown

P.S. Don't forget to visit the website at www.HHESecrets.com. It is full of more tips, interviews from experts, and resources to help you along the way. Every chapter has a QR code that will take you right to the website. Simply use your handheld digital device (iPad, phone, etc.) to scan the code. You can download a reader for free in the application store of your service provider by searching "QR code reader." Enjoy!

Stress Is Inevitable, So Why Should I Care?

The Power of YOU

I've experienced the scary symptoms of stress firsthand and have worked with people who are suffering in so many ways because of stress. But I've also experienced and witnessed firsthand the life-transforming power that stress management can have on health, relationships, productivity, and overall happiness. Stress *is* inevitable, but it doesn't have to take you down. YOU have the power to change your relationship to stress. YOU have the power to minimize stress. YOU have the power to maximize your own life simply by the choices you make.

Right now, you have a choice to make. Will you continue to be paralyzed by stress and remain a slave to your fear and to-do lists or will you join me as we journey down this path to less stress together? I promise you that if you come along with me, if you use the secrets I will outline in this book, and if you explore all of the resources out there to reduce your stress, you *will* see amazing changes in your life. By joining me in this Stress Less Revolution you are making a commitment to yourself and your loved ones that you value and respect yourself and them so much, you are willing to learn, change, and grow—all with the goal of minimizing your stress and maximizing your life for the foreseeable future.

Are you ready to take the leap? Are you finally ready to take back control of your life so you can live a life of greater happiness and better health? Do you want to write your own life story that includes fun, relaxation, productivity, and less stress? YES, YES, and YES! Now is your time to make the changes you have wanted to make for so long. And now, you have an easy, enjoyable, and powerful tool to make it happen—this book! Every chapter, every sentence, and every single word has been constructed with you in mind. Life is busy. Life can be hard. But I have structured this book so that you can quickly start to make changes in as little as a few seconds. The framework I have built is one that is completely life-oriented and customizable for you.

Every one of the secrets I share in this book is powerful, but I'm not asking you to internalize and learn every one. I'm not even asking you to pick one and do everything I suggest. Instead, I am laying out multiple options per chapter. Every option is listed at the end of the chapter in a super-simple grid so you can see which ones you can start right now and which ones take a little longer to put into action. You can see which ones are fun, which are easy, and which are most important. With just one glance you can pick and choose the stress-busting secrets that feel most natural and comfortable for your lifestyle, from an instant stress reliever like a hug to a longer term stress reliever like shifting your food choices over time. And to help you make the right choices, we'll start by laying the foundation for you so that you can logically, spiritually, and physically pick the right stress reducers that will fit your goals.

The key is to keep moving ahead while experimenting with the tips that sound the most appealing for you. The ideas that you choose to use will not be the same as the ones that your neighbor or even your spouse will choose. The path to less stress is a very personal journey, which requires an open mind and an open heart. Some of the suggestions may seem very foreign to you, but remember that different doesn't mean you shouldn't try them. The more willing you are to be open to change and stretching out of your comfort zone in the process, the more likely you are to succeed *and* make some interesting and fun memories in the process. Plus, by getting used to new experiences and change, you are becoming stronger and more resilient to stress.

And so I go back to YOU! As you embark on this adventure into new ways of thinking about stress, happiness, and health, there will be times you'll be pushed out of your comfort zone. You will experience fear and anxiety. You will tell yourself it won't work. You will be unwilling to try something new. All of these are normal and okay. Change is a major driver of stress because anything that upsets our normal routine and comfort level in our little world is scary. In fact, you may actually experience stress on this path to less stress. I know, I know. That doesn't seem right. But over time and with practice, you will get more comfortable with change and in the process, also experience much less stress. YOU have the control over your destiny. So embrace your power, and let's make this happen!

No More Excuses

I can't tell you how many times I've heard the excuses:

"Everyone experiences stress."
"There's nothing I can do about it."
"Stress is inevitable."
"My stress will never go away. It's just a part of life."

Yes—stress *is* inevitable, but that doesn't mean we should just sit by and let it impact our lives in negative ways. If we had that attitude, life would get filled up by crummy stuff pretty quickly. It's up to YOU to take control of the stress in your life so you can live a happier and healthier life. But why? If stress is indeed inevitable, what's the point in working so hard to get it under control? It just sounds like more work and more stress.

There are thousands of research studies showing the negative implications of stress on our lives. Every day TV shows air around the world and articles are published in magazines, newspapers, books, and online to help us relax and release stress. From mental strain to relationship problems to physical disease, stress symptoms impact every area of our lives. And yet, despite the alarming findings and the sky-rocketing use of antianxiety and antidepressant prescription drugs, we continue to let stress overtake our lives both at work and in our everyday lives.

Many people think stress is just in our heads or that it is caused by the brain. While there is some truth to that, stress is more than just a mental affliction. Our perception of the things that happen to us in our lives is the driver of how our brains *and* bodies will respond. For example, being stuck in traffic can be frustrating, and it's a common problem that stresses us out. Our daily commute is a grind and starts and ends the work day in a negative way, thus setting the tone for our whole day—not just the time we are sitting in the car. Imagine sitting in stalled traffic. The cars around you not moving. People trying to merge in. The minutes ticking by, pushing you one step closer to being late. And then some jerk comes flying past from the on ramp and sneaks into the stopped line of cars several cars up, "winning" the race to get where he's going faster than you. You feel your anger rise as your hands clench the steering wheel. You might start to sweat as your heart beats faster. We've all been there. Traffic can be stressful. But what actually happens that causes that anger and stress to set in when all we are doing is sitting there?

What Is the Stress Response?

Without going biology-geek on you (I was pre-med for a while and love a good science lesson), the stress response is an important and complicated physical response that kicks in when a stressor is impending. In the caveman days, that might have been a saber-toothed tiger or other scary beast. When that tiger approached, that caveman knew he had to either fight it or get away from it to avoid harm or even death. Thus the term "fight or flight response," which is often used when explaining what happens to us when we are stressed. Upon seeing the tiger, the caveman's brain says, "Hey, there is danger. Let's fight or fly." That message signals the adrenal glands and other parts of the body to release stress chemicals like prostaglandins, leukotrienes, cortisol, and adrenaline, which kick our body into high gear to prepare us for what is to come next—either a battle with the tiger or running like hell to escape it.

When the stress chemicals begin to circulate, they increase blood pressure, heart rate, perspiration, and respiration and slow down nonessential bodily functions. This is why you feel the rush of sensation when you almost get in a car accident or when the phone rings in the middle of the night. Your body senses impending danger that could potentially harm you and acts instantly to help protect you from it. That's why you become sweaty, breathe harder, and feel almost lightheaded when a big stress hits. As soon as the stress disappears (the caveman kills the tiger or escapes to safety), his body returns to its happy place (or homeostasis, if you want the scientific word). As the stress chemicals are circulated out of his body, his heart rate returns to normal, his blood pressure drops, he stops sweating, and his breathing regulates. He goes back to hunting and gathering until the next stress appears, and the stress response starts all over again. He knows how to heed the warning system and do what he's supposed to do to manage the stress—fight or flee.

In the short term, this stress response is a very, very good thing. You want it to get activated by threats to your well-being. It is our internal alarm system to protect us. The problem today is that sabertoothed tigers aren't out there stalking us. True danger is very unlikely in our lives. Yet we are allowing things like traffic, tough days at work, and busy schedules to unnecessarily stress us out. We aren't heeding our body's signals to us that stress is impending, so it keeps on releasing stress chemicals until we take notice and do something to change it—again to fight or flee.

When the stress response is continually activated, those stress chemicals are circulating in us at low levels all the time. This everpresent cocktail of chemicals causes damage in the process. Cortisol and adrenaline aren't meant to be active in our bodies all the time. They are supposed to be released on an as-needed basis—short jolts of energy to prompt us to take action. Ignoring the signs of stress forces your body to keep releasing those stress chemicals in hopes that you will finally notice the symptoms that they produce and do something to protect yourself. As they circulate, your body systems and organs down to your very cells are bathed in these chemicals. This is not a good thing because as this happens, the cell walls are actually damaged in the process. The damage that occurs to the cells causes inflammation that is linked to illness and the leading causes of death in the United States.

When you think of inflammation, you may think about a swollen ankle after a twist or a blister that forms after wearing a bad pair of shoes. The area gets red, becomes hot, and may fill with fluid. The injury to the body causes a response that helps heal and protect the area from further damage. Blood flow to the area is increased to speed healing, and prostaglandins and leukotrienes (inflammatory-causing hormones) are released, which cause the pain, heat, and redness. The stress response works similarly in that stress also prompts the release of prostaglandins and leukotrienes. To help counteract these proinflammatory chemicals, our bodies pump out cortisol. If you don't take action to reduce stress, the body keeps pumping out this host of chemicals, and they continue to do damage in the body, which can manifest as illness and long-term disease.

Yikes! That is a lot of stuff going on in our bodies that we don't even realize. And this response doesn't just happen when big stuff comes along like the death of a loved one, a bad day at work, or a health scare. This stress response is activated for even the smallest of stressors like traffic or a minor disagreement with a loved one. We inadvertently sabotage our own health and happiness simply by ignoring the system that is there to protect us. But we can learn to notice the alarm when it goes off and stop the stress response before it causes damage.

Once you figure out what your own personal stress cues are, there are thousands of resources out in the world and hundreds of ideas and tips right here in this book and on our website to help you have a less-stressed, happier, and healthier life. Sorting through all of them can be overwhelming if you don't know how to pick the right one for you. To get you started in a positive way, I will outline a process for deciding which goals to pursue first, and more importantly, a process for making our big dreams and small goals a reality.

Getting Started

Most big goals begin and end in short order. Diet plans, New Year's resolutions, quitting smoking, home projects, lifestyle changes—you have the best intentions at the beginning, but pretty soon you're cheating a little here, regressing a little there. Why is that? Why can't we commit to changes for more than a few weeks, even if it's for our own good? There are many deeper reasons for abandoning goals that are individual to everyone's situations, but one of the common overarching causes of failing to make changes is because it is too much pressure to follow through on such lofty expectations of ourselves in such a compacted space of time. When we impose on ourselves a structured goal with an expectation that we will change our entire life to meet that goal, it is completely unrealistic and sucks all of our energy into that one focus, leaving the other aspects of our life ignored and left behind. That isn't the way to accomplish goals for ourselves. Instead, we need to first pinpoint exactly what and why we want to change and then come up with the best way for YOU to implement those changes. If you want to lose weight because you want to look better and be healthier, that is great. But without some background on why those things are important and how that goal fits into YOUR life, it is unlikely you will find a system that works for you. If you envision a less-stressed life for you and your family, that is fantastic, but you must have a more focused plan of attack to make it happen.

Happy Hour Effect's approach to goal setting can help you find your way. It can help you understand yourself better so you know where and how to focus your efforts so your goals are more easily achievable in a way that works for you. Whether it's more effective stress management or another goal you have for yourself, you must have a deep desire to make a change that helps solve a burning problem you have in your life—and you must want to do it for yourself, not for your spouse or anyone else. If you don't have that attitude, you will fail.

With this book, you don't have to follow a step-by-step, one-size-fits-all plan. Instead, we will help you use your own strengths and weaknesses to develop a plan that fits into YOUR life. It's a flexible, fun, and actionable process of connecting with yourself and finding your harmony in a way that best fits YOUR needs. We will provide you the framework, tools, and ideas to find the realistic path to less stress and a better life that works for you.

What Are GOALS?

Inherently we know what goals are: things we want to accomplish. But there is much more to goal setting than just having something you want to happen in your life. Yet the old goal setting trap snares us every time. They all come with desired outcomes that suck us in for a while, but then life gets busy and our once-so-important goals fall to the bottom of the priority list. Sadly, this failure to achieve or even attempt our dreams can lead to stress. Those goals we have sit lodged in the back of our minds, always wanting us to take action. But the anxiety of another to-do on the list takes up our energy instead.

I have a dream of producing a documentary film that has been bouncing around in my head for about three years. Every once in awhile I come across a note or idea I've jotted down in a notebook, and it reminds me of this unfulfilled dream just sitting there waiting to take shape. It taunts me—and not in a good way. I spend hours deliberating over it instead of taking action. And while it's a good dream, it's one that is causing me stress because I'm not doing anything with it. So many of us have dreams like this—big ideas that we want to accomplish but do nothing to make a reality.

The secret to making your goals a reality is to have a benchmark to use to decide if a goal fits your needs and lifestyle. If you don't have enough pain in your life to drive you to want to make a change, you won't be motivated to work on the goal. The Happy Hour Effect approach to GOALS helps to identify pain and determine if a goal will work for you. Here are the steps involved:

- **Gut-Checked:** The goal "feels" right. You know in your gut that it is the right thing to do, and it energizes you. You know you have the pain in your life that makes reaching the goal a true necessity that can't be pushed off any longer. Fear may be present about undertaking the goal, but the potential for success if you reach the goal overrides that fear.

- **Obtainable:** The goal isn't so lofty that you can never achieve it. It is something you can reach in a reasonable amount of time with reasonable amounts of effort.

- **Actionable:** The goal is able to be reached by solid, tangible actions you can take in your life right now. It isn't so complicated that you can't put simple action steps into a plan to reach it. And I reinforce right now: you should be able to take even a tiny step to making the goal a reality in just minutes, even if it's as simple as doing a search online or reading a book about your goal.

- **Life-Oriented:** The goal meshes with your day-to-day life. It fits into your family dynamic, your current reality, and your future dreams. It is a goal that is easily implemented into your schedule. You will have the support you need to make it happen.

- **Small Steps:** The goal can be broken down into tiny steps that build upon one another to get you to the end goal. The main goal may be to find a better job, but the mini steps might be: decide on next job targets, update resume, write cover letters, research companies, send out resumes, etc. And even those mini steps can be broken down further into even smaller steps. The smaller the goal, the easier it is to accomplish quickly and easily.

All of these criteria should be met if GOALS are to be successful. If you set goals that are unreachable, it will only make you feel more unbalanced. You will feel disheartened and may even feel like a failure. The key is to build plans that involve realistic goals that act as stepping stones to get you to where you want to be in the future.

Here is an example: If you have a goal of changing careers and starting your own scrapbooking business, it is not realistic to think you can quit your job tomorrow and the money will start flowing in next week. Instead, you need to begin with small goals to help you reach the bigger goal of starting your own business. Your goals might look like this:

1. Start researching the scrapbooking industry. What are annual sales in the industry? Who are the big manufacturers? Who are the core customers? What are they buying? Where are scrapbooking materials and classes sold? Get into those stores and visit those websites. Learn all you can about your goal. If you are armed with knowledge, it will help you all along the path to reaching the bigger goal.

2. Attend scrapbooking tradeshows and events. Start to build contacts and learn how the industry works. Join business networking organizations and start to build a network that can help you once you take the leap into business ownership down the road.

3. Get your own finances in order. Meet with a financial planner to talk about your goals and ideas. He/she will help you put into action the best way to achieve the financial stability and resources to make your goals a reality. And they can help you build a timeline based on your financial situation. You may need to save for another year or two before things can happen.

4. Start getting experience in the industry. Work part-time at a scrapbooking or craft store. Find a scrapbooking company that may want a sales rep or other position that will give you insider information on the industry.

5. Start brainstorming for your business plan. What is your business name and logo? Who are your customers going to be? How will you finance it? Who will design your website and marketing materials? How will you build the business (advertising, tradeshows, etc.)?

This list can go on and on, but you see what I mean by building a list of small goals that will all culminate into bigger goals. This isn't an easy task—especially if your goal is really big. But if you just dive in and start working toward it, it will inspire you to keep moving along. That is the key to success in making any goal or dream a reality.

In the case of stress management and this book, it is the same process. As you read through each chapter, use the GOALS criteria (gut-checked, obtainable, actionable, life-oriented, small steps) to help you decide if that specific suggestion will work for your life. You don't need to use every one, and in fact, it's better if you just start with one or two ideas from the book. Each chapter is laid out simply with a brief introduction to the secret, the nitty gritty good stuff with ideas for changes you can make for less stress, health and happiness, sidebars with insight from experts, next steps, and an action grid at the end of each chapter.

These action grids are my favorite feature of the book. They give you a quick visual reference of all the ideas from that chapter and tell you what it will take to achieve each one. Each grid tells you if the idea is easy, requires a little effort, or is hard. It tells you if the idea is fun, easy, or super important. And it tells you how long it will take to implement the idea and experience a difference in your life (from instant to a month). The grids are an easy and powerful reference you can use whenever you need or want to experience less stress or need a boost to your health or happiness. Printable versions of these grids are also available on the website so you can keep them in your planner or at your desk for quick access.

Don't be afraid to experiment and let the ideas come in and out of your life over time. One solution that works for you right now might not work next year after something changes in your life. Our existence is fluid and ever-changing, and our wellness practices should flex too. Be open to these winds of change and you will be better prepared to deal with the big and small stresses of life. Now that you know how to use GOALS to decide which direction to take on your stress-less journey, let's get down to brass tacks.

The Happy Hour Effect Life Map

Before throwing out a bunch of ideas to you on how to minimize stress and maximize life, I want to give you a powerful visual framework to help guide you. Every idea in this book and on the website, and any that you will encounter in the future, falls into one of five Life Map Zones.

- Core Life—these are the most important, core things in your life like kids, significant other, friends, spirituality, and health.

- Passions & Commitments—these are things that you do just for the fun (or not so fun) of it to help yourself and others, like hobbies, committees, and travel.

- Work—this is anything you do for financial security, including working for others, side jobs, or self-employment.

- Challenges—these are the big roadblocks that arise and hold you back, like death of a loved one, disease, relationship problems, bad habits, or past issues.

- Dreams—these are those big, crazy goals you have that you lie awake dreaming about, like a dream vacation, writing a book, starting a business, or any other exciting idea.

I use these classifications as part of a process I developed called Life Mapping. It is an exercise I do with groups and individuals to help them visually see all of the moving pieces of their lives. By laying all of the responsibilities and tasks of your life out into each Life Map Zone and identifying the drivers of your emotions, you can pretty quickly and easily see areas that stress you out and areas that energize you. People so often assume they are just generally stressed, but when we dig in and do this exercise, they realize that their life is actually pretty amazing; just one area is causing them stress that's carrying over into the other areas. I recommend that you go to the website and print out a blank Life Map and do your own. It's super easy but extremely powerful. You can see in the sample Life Map that it's a simple fill-in-the-blanks exercise where you list out all of the things in your life that fit into each Life Map Zone. A step-by-step overview is on the website if you need more specific directions.

There are no right or wrong items to put on the map. You may have just one or two things under each Life Map Zone, or you might need more space. The Life Map is simply a way for you to see all of the things that contribute to your life at any given time. I highly recommend that you do this exercise before reading the book. And be honest with yourself. Don't leave things off the map because they seem silly, unrealistic, or embarrassing. No one will see your Life Map except you, unless you choose to share it. And remember that your Life Map will change often as you add new activities, your relationships shift, you encounter new challenges, or you change jobs.

This book is organized so each of the twelve secrets is classified into one of the five Life Map Zones. This allows you to immediately get to work on any parts of your life that need extra attention. For example, I had a client who worked as a nurse and had a side business of selling items on eBay. Through the Life Mapping exercise, she found that her nursing job was extremely stressful, while she loved every minute of her side business. We worked on getting her work stress under control and building in GOALS to make her eBay business a bigger part of her life. Personally, I use my Life Map almost daily. I check in to see what is causing me stress at any given time, then I use ideas that

Life Map

Challenges

Diabetes

Fights with mother-in-law

Home maintenance

Rising debt

Passions & Commitments

Things that take the most time go on the left in the bigger boxes while smaller tasks and responsibilities go on the right in the smaller boxes.

Gardening

School committee

Carpool

Yoga class

Volunteering

Travel

Church

Movies

Lake home

Reading

Book club

Pets

Core Life

You

Children

Sleep

Home

Spouse

Health

Relatives

Work & Money

Account manager

Dreams

Start scrapbooking business

Pay off credit card debt

Finish master's degree

My first goal to change is:

My affirmation is:

Circle the items that energize and inspire you.

Put an X through the items that stress you out the most.

Minimize Stress, Maximize Life • HappyHourEffect.com • kristen@happyhoureffect.com specifically focus on that Life Map Zone to minimize the stress and boost health and happiness. As you work on your own Life Map, you will find your own Life Map Zones that need work and then go right to that corresponding secret in the book. For example, if you discover you need to make bigger strides to making a big dream come true, you would go right to the Dreams Life Map Zone and use tips from one of the secrets that fall into that area.

Are you ready to take action and make changes in your life? If you're still a little worried that this will be too hard or that there is too much to change, take a moment now to think about why you are afraid. Most likely it is for a few different reasons:

- Not sure what will happen after change **(fear of future)**
- Not confident in skills/abilities to handle new responsibilities **(fear of failure)**
- Don't **trust** the leader (you can trust me!)
- Afraid of **loss, isolation, and loneliness** as you implement new changes
- Don't know what people will think of you if you change **(fear of others' judgments)**
- Plus a million other excuses and reasons we will fabricate to avoid change

Believe me, I've heard *every* excuse out there to avoid change. I've made most of those excuses myself. It's okay to be scared or unsure of yourself when you decide to make changes in your life. The most important thing is that you pick the right tips (go back and read the *Getting Started* chapter for review on GOALS), get support from others, have a plan, and enjoy the ride. If you try to make changes but become miserable, you aren't following your gut. If your goals are too big, they aren't obtainable. If no one is supporting you, they aren't life-oriented. Every day, do a mini check-in with yourself to see how you're doing, and don't be afraid to try something new. I promise you that it will benefit you and make you more resilient to change and the stress that goes along with it.

Each Life Map Zone includes multiple secrets that relate to improving your life in that area. Here is an overview:

1. **Challenges**: I begin with this Life Map Zone because this is often where many of the big roadblocks come from. The pain and stress of past loss, tough situations, and emotional upsets can pop up unexpectedly and throw us off our game. Challenges in life often cause us to victimize or feel sorry for ourselves. We fall into the woe-is-me mindset, and pretty soon life is spiraling downward and stress blows up in our face. This Life Map Zone includes:
   - Secret #1—Quit Your Bitchin'!
   - Secret #2—Check, Check, aaaand Check

2. **Work**: This is another area that causes much of the stress in our lives. Research shows that work and economic factors top the list of reasons for stress. Tough bosses, job loss, debt, and differences in money mindset can cause anxiety and stress for even the most resilient. This Life Map Zone includes:
   - Secret #3—I Love My Job (sarcastic laugh)
   - Secret #4—Money, Money, Money

3. **Core Life**: This Life Map Zone is really the most important one to keep aligned. Unfortunately, factors from the other zones often push these out of whack. However, there are things you can do to fortify yourself and your loved ones from the damage of stress, while boosting your happiness and health in the process. This Life Map Zone includes:
   - Secret #5—Family Matters
   - Secret #6—Operation Body
   - Secret #7—Sleep & Sex for Less Stress

4. **Passions and Commitments**: In this Life Map Zone, we do things for fun, relaxation, and enjoyment, or we participate in activities that help others. It can also include things we do

out of duty or because we feel someone else expects us to do them. It is important that the tasks that help others also fulfill us in the process so they don't stress us out unnecessarily. This Life Map Zone includes:

- Secret #8—Stress and the Uglies
- Secret #9—Ohm Is for Everyone
- Secret #10—Hair, Poop, and Feedings (sounds stressful)

5. **Dreams**: This is the exciting Life Map Zone, which can really get our juices flowing. But if we let our dreams sit unfulfilled for too long without taking action on them, they can eventually begin to cause us stress. This Life Map Zone includes:

- Secret #11—Me-Time for Less Stress
- Secret #12—Cross It Off the Bucket List

As you go through each secret within the Life Map Zones, have your Life Map handy so you can relate it directly back to your own life. The more personal and customized you can be in your approach to stress, the higher your chances of success. Are you ready? Here we go!

I.

Challenges

Resources:

Get downloadable worksheets and
tutorials for Secret #1
Quit Your Bitchin' at:

HHESecrets.com

*Use your smartphone to scan the below
QR code to go there now.*

Benefits:

- People will like you more.
- You will like others more.
- You will feel less anxious over the stresses in your life.
- As a positive person instead of a negative one, people will relate to you differently.
- You will wake up feeling energized and happy to be alive despite the challenges you face.
- It will be easier to work towards your goals and dreams without the roadblock of negative self-talk.
- Your relationships with others will feel more open and natural, leading to more intimacy and shared experiences.
- What goes around comes around! Bring joy to others and it will come back to you!

Secret #1
Quit Your Bitchin'!

Why Complaining, Self-Pity, Victimization,
Nagging, Whining, and Feeling Sorry for
Yourself Won't Get You Anywhere

"A loving person lives in a loving world. A hostile person lives in a hostile world: everyone you meet is your mirror." —Ken Keyes Jr.

"I am a part of all that I have met." —Alfred, Lord Tennyson

What's on Tap?

The least popular person in any room is the buzzkill who sucks the life from the party. It's the same friend whose Facebook posts chronicle their latest disappointment in life or the malady that they woke up with that morning. I'm guilty of posts like this myself and have to snap myself back to reality when I realize I'm causing negativity not only in myself, but for everyone who just read my poor-me post. And I am not alone. Everyone is guilty of causing themselves stress and creating their own drama at one time or another—but some are much better (or worse) at it than others. We can all name a few Debbie Downers in our life. Maybe it's even you. And yet, the poor-me mindset continues despite some easy fixes that can take us from totally stressed to totally blessed in just moments.

The Happy Hour Effect Secret #1 will help us quit bringing on our own anxiety that arises when we bitch, complain, nag, whine, and generally, become a pain in the rear to everyone around us. By spinning our negativity into more positive ways of walking in the world, we can be less stressed, healthier, and happier. We will learn:

- Why victimizing ourselves creates stress
- What we can do to honestly look at our own stress-creating habits
- Why we should cultivate relationships that will enrich us instead of drain us
- Why to show gratitude for what we have instead of complaining about what we don't
- How to maintain perspective in the face of stress

All of these things are the foundation to the Happy Hour Effect mindset. By starting with these important elements that spin our self-stress habits into self-growth, it will give us a positive springboard to launch into the secrets that follow.

Why Do We Bitch?

When the going gets tough, our natural response is to armor ourselves against the challenge by saying and thinking things like:

"What did I do to deserve this?"
"The world is out to get me."
"It wasn't my fault."
"I'm cursed."
"I have terrible luck."

The list could go on and on. Very rarely do we say, "This crappy thing happened, but now I'm going to take responsibility and change things for myself." That would mean admitting we had some hand in causing our own problems. No one wants to be the bearer of their own bad tidings. So instead, we reach out to others with our theories on why life has been so unkind to us, sucking them into our negativity pit in the process.

Going back to the Facebook example, think about the posts that are negative. Someone says they're having a bad day, and what happens? All of their virtual friends post words of encouragement to make the person feel better. That's all good, right? But for just a moment, that negative post pulled all those people down with it. Human nature is to feel empathy and pain for the person in pain. I'm not saying that is a bad thing, but what if you could spare others from having to feel that pain in the first place by skipping that negative post? Makes you think, doesn't it?

We can all name a friend or two who suck the life from every party or happy hour. They are the ones who show up and then launch into their dissatisfaction with their weight, their job, their love life— it's always something. Again—maybe this person is you. And what happens? Everyone in the group reassures Mr. Unhappy or Ms. Less-Than-Cheery that life is good, everything will be okay, and they are good people. Instead of taking action to lose weight, find a new job, or instill some spice into their love life, they seek out the temporary bandage of the empathetic ears of friends. Again, it's not a bad thing. But what if that happy hour was about fun and happiness instead of complaining and stress?

It's hard to pull ourselves out of the self-pity rut, especially when we don't know or won't admit that we're in it. But for just a few minutes, let's get real and pinpoint your own habits that cause you stress.

What Can I Do to Stop My Whining?

When you think back to very stressful times in your life, didn't it seem like whatever could have gone wrong, did? It is a self-fulfilling prophecy when we continually moan and whine about how the world is kicking us when we're down or that the universe is just plain out to get us. If we think that is the case, then it will be so. But in reality, nothing is out to get you. YOU are the only thing hurting yourself by the reactions you have to stress.

In fact, not only do you bring yourself down when you bemoan your sorry state of affairs, but you negatively impact the people around you and stress them out on top of the stress you are causing yourself. But there are steps you can take to begin to control those self-sabotaging voices in your head and spin them into a positive force that will help you feel less stress and more harmony in all of the areas of your life.

First and foremost, you *must* be honest with yourself. No one wants to admit that they are a whiner or causing their own stress. But there are many people out there who spend more time in negative mode instead of maintaining a positive state of mind. And this negativity sets the stage for extreme stress. Start with this review of your interactions:

1. Think back on your conversations with others over the last few weeks. Have they been upbeat, positive chats or negative, complaint-filled bitch sessions? What percent have been positive versus negative?

2. Review the negative conversations. Who were they with? What were you talking about? How long did the conversation last? What was the outcome or action item from the conversation? If the bummer conversations are with the same person over and over, it's time to reevaluate that relationship. If it's always on the same topic, it's time to gain some perspective. If you walked away from the conversation without an action item to help solve the problem, then it was truly just a bitch session with no real value. It's time to spin your discussions into more therapeutic, healing conversations that set the stage for positive change instead of perpetuation of the negativity.

3. Are you sucking others into your drama when you don't need to? Do you vent and complain to family, friends, and cowork-

Giving Thanks Through Stress

by Lee Blum, eating disorder survivor
and author of *Accidental Peace*

Stress—the inevitable effect of being present in this world.

I used to deal with stress in a highly ineffective way—one that hurt me and hurt others around me. Without appropriate coping skills and with a predisposition to addictive behavior, I found a drug that numbed me out—numbed me from dealing with the stress of life. Instead of coping by feeling, I coped by not feeling and in return abused myself and my body. I starved myself as a way to run away. It wasn't conscious—it was what was available. I didn't know another way because the pain was too much, the stress too overwhelming, and the fear too great.

It led me to my deathbed where I was forced to make a choice—a choice to learn to deal with life in an effective way, to fight my addiction, or risk the grave or a body that would no longer cooperate. An eating disorder is not a choice, but recovery is. I began making the choices to face life, to find alternative coping skills, and to deal with my stress. We all have it: the stress. You can't run from it, because eventually it will find you.

What did I do? I reached out for help. All the time. From friends to therapists to coworkers. I shared my feelings, I talked through my pain, and I told people when I was scared. I also broke plates. Hundreds of plates smashed into tiny little pieces. This helped me stop taking the anger and fear out on my body and instead physically releasing it into the plates. I only did this for a few months until I was able to tolerate my own distress better. But I knew it was better to take it out on a plate rather than my own body. It has been sixteen years since I began walking down the road of recovery. Life is still overwhelming and can be stressful. I have three kids, work part-time at an eating disorder facility, write blogs, and am writing a book. What do I do now? Now I rely on my toolbox of coping skills. First I take time in my quiet space and pray. Sometimes I pray out loud, sometimes I journal. Second I make sure I get enough sleep, as I make wiser decisions when I am well rested. And third I practice gratitude, where I make lists all over of what I am grateful for, whether it is the bird outside the window, a hug from my child, or just the gratitude of having lungs that work. Gratitude settles me and refocuses me to the present moment. When I am in the present moment, I don't have to think forward or backwards. I can just be. And then I thank God I am alive. And that is enough.

Lee Blum is a speaker and author on eating disorders and addictions. She works as a health educator at the Melrose Institute for Eating Disorders, working with patients who have dual diagnosis of chemical dependency and eating disorders. Her memoir, *Accidental Peace*, will be published in Spring 2013 by InterVarsity Press. Lee blogs at: findingbalance.com and gurze.com ers about your problems that don't impact them? If so, you are only bringing them down and forcing unnecessary stress into their lives. If you are truly seeking them out for counsel and advice on how to move forward and fix the challenge, continue that. But if it is the same conversation over and over and only YOU spend the bulk of the time talking, it is a worthless conversation that is only hurting yourself and others.

4. Do you move forward when challenges arise and not let yourself get stuck in that problem, or do you let yourself dwell on it and go over and over it with yourself and others? If you can't learn to move ahead when tough situations get you down, it is time for some perspective and a change in attitude.

If you read through the above questions and answered honestly, chances are a few of them were hard to admit. No one wants to be the source of their own unhappiness. But the good news is that you *can* make changes, and that is where we're headed next. As you review the following tips and ideas to stop causing yourself drama, be sure you are picking and choosing the ones that fit most with your life and situation. And don't try to do it all at once. Take small steps and you will get to a place of positivity and forward momentum in your life.

How Can I Change My Relationships So They're Less Stressful?

This is a tough one. Many of us are in relationships with others that can't be changed. Family, friends, spouses, and coworkers can be difficult sometimes (or all the time) but can be hard to let go of—especially family relationships. But we can change the dynamic of those relationships with just a few quick shifts in your communication style:

1. Suggest Solutions: If you spend the bulk of your time with someone complaining, nagging, or whining, either about their behavior or about your own life, take a time out from that relationship and evaluate what this person really does for you. If it's a spouse, is he or she really as bad as you think, or are you projecting some unhappiness of your own onto them? What did you love about them when you first met? Try to re-capture that essence again. Admit your own faults and weaknesses and move forward with a fresh start. If it's a friend, change the course of conversations you have with him or her. When things start to go negative, spin it into a more positive direction. If a girlfriend is complaining about her appearance, change the subject to what she can do to feel more beautiful and pampered, like a spa day or new hairstyle. If it's a family member complaining about their job, instead of letting them go on and on about how awful it is, suggest ways he or she can try something new, or suggest other job opportunities that might be out there. **Every complaining/whining/nagging conversation should always be shifted to find a solution to the problem. It should never be one long bitch session.**

2. **Keep It Short:** Venting feels good. If you've had a bad day, let it out to a trusted friend or partner. But once you've quickly shared your frustrations and feelings, let it go and change the subject to more uplifting conversation. It may be difficult sometimes, but instead of pulling the other person into your unhappiness and wrecking their time with you, leave the negativity behind and move on to something you both enjoy. This will reduce your stress and prevent the other person from going down the path of stress with you.

Teresa had a spouse who would come home from work and solely complain all night and all weekend about how much he hated his job. From the moment he walked in the door, Teresa and their kids knew to leave Dad alone because he was stressed out about his job. They would go on family outings without him, or if he did come, he would end up ruining the whole thing because of his attitude and crankiness about his job. I suggested to Teresa that instead of treading on eggshells around her husband, she talk to him about how his behavior was affecting the family and stressing them all out. Teresa did just that and talked to him about how we cause our own stress. Once he was made aware that his actions were making everyone around him even more stressed out than he was, he changed his attitude. It took some time, but after a month, he was back to his normal self. He still disliked his job, but the shift in his home life was so great that it prompted him to seek out a different job.

Of course, not every person will react so positively or quickly to a suggestion for change. In fact, many people get defensive, saying, "You just don't understand how bad it is." They truly believe they have it worse than anyone else out there. They require some serious perspective-shifting work, and it isn't always successful. But starting small is the first step to change. **So when you need to vent or complain, keep it short and go positive from there.**

3. **Regain Control:** When stress sets in, it's usually because of some change happening in our lives. This change makes us feel out of control, and when we lose control, we tend to enter the "bitching zone." When parts of our life start to spin away from us, we start to complain and put up that armor of self-defense. When something goes wrong in our life, whether it's work, money, relationships, health, or any of the other millions of things we juggle, the best thing to do is to switch from reactive to proactive mode. Instead of going into that poor-me mentality and just assuming crap is going to happen, we need to take action to change the situation.

So many of us have bad things happen, and we just stagnate.

We get stuck in stress and dwell on it until nothing else matters. We define our existence by something bad that happened in the past. But if we can change that mindset and instead use stress as a springboard for positive change, we can reduce and even eliminate the stress as we take action to counteract it. I like to say it's time to get proactive instead of reactive, meaning that instead of just letting come what may, we take life by the horns and steer it in the direction we want it to go. If you were fired and can't find a new job, start your own business, launch a blog, or volunteer. **Do *something*! Don't just rest on your laurels and assume things will just happen the way they should happen. Take action, be proactive, and regain control of the flow of your life.**

One of the most difficult challenges and biggest stressors in life is dealing with other people's crap. We are human beings who empathize, sympathize, take on others' problems, and want to take away pain. But sometimes, to preserve our own sanity, health, and happiness, we need to restructure our relationships with others and get the other person (or ourselves) on a new path that doesn't suck others down too.

Why Should I Show More Gratitude and Kindness?

Flipping the switch from resentful to thankful isn't easy, especially when we're lying in that pit of self-pity. But research shows that cultivating a lifestyle of gratitude does change the happiness levels we experience throughout life. And of course, happiness really does negate stress because we feel more in control, less fearful, and more hopeful about our life's path.

The very best suggestion I have seen for becoming more gracious is to journal about it every day, or even better, to make it a public change so you are getting others onto the gratitude bandwagon with you. Just

The Gift in the Gunk: Transforming Life's Droppings into Blessings

by Theresa Rose, HoopWoman™ and award-winning author

Gunk. It's that unwelcome icky stuff in our lives that can wreak havoc on us if we aren't careful. Anything from traffic jams to the loss of a loved one can be characterized as gunk, a life situation that we would not have chosen if given the chance. Unprocessed gunk can morph into chronic stress and other nasty physical and emotional manifestations if it's ignored long enough. However, when you develop a conscious relationship with your gunk, you will soon discover the hidden gems contained within it.

Here are a few ways you can be prepared when the gunk inevitably arises:

1. **Self care.** When times are tough, it's not the time to skimp on taking care of yourself. When your tank is empty, you won't have enough energy to handle things appropriately. Make a commitment to yourself to stop being a martyr and start honoring your vehicle. Get more sleep. Eat better. Move. Play. Get quiet. Ask for what you need.

2. **Be in it.** When the spam is really hitting the fan, our tendency is to want to escape. Don't do it! Even though it's painful, don't try to check out or numb yourself through self-medication. Drowning yourself in alcohol, drugs, sugar, TV, or the Internet will only make the gunk that much more difficult when you eventually emerge from your self-induced emotional coma.

3. **Take a gratitude bath.** Taking a moment on a regular basis to acknowledge all of the wonderful things in your life, both past and present, will minimize the sting of any situation. Flood your mind and heart with all that is good in your world. You have breath! You have enough food and clean water! You have adequate shelter! You have love! No matter the troubles you face, you are rich beyond measure.

Once you have a strong foundation, you can look at the difficulties through a new lens. If you are struggling with money, maybe you are also prioritizing what's really important and letting go of what is no longer needed. If you are facing a major loss, the gift may be the tremendous love and learning you have gained as a result of having had it in your life. As Dr. Seuss said, "Don't cry because it's over. Smile because it happened."

By reorienting ourselves to our gunk, we recognize that everything, *absolutely everything*, contains a juicy gift. When you flip gunk on its head and see the positive elements as well as the negative, you will go from living a life of pain to one filled with joy.

Theresa "Hoop Woman™" Rose is a national motivational humorist and award-winning author of *Opening the Kimono: A Woman's Intimate Journey Through Life's Biggest Challenges*. Her mission is to help people rediscover their unlimited power, and her favorite teacher is her beloved hula hoop. Discover more at TheresaRose.com.

a sentence or two per day on Facebook, Twitter, or a blog, or a few words written in a notebook or planner, can shift how you are perceived by others and how you look at the world. Imagine if everyone shared one thing every day on Facebook that they were thankful for. Wouldn't your News Feed be a much happier place?

In addition to gratitude, what if every day you did something nice for someone else without expecting something in return? Think back to a time when you held the door for someone or let someone go in front of you in line at the grocery store. Felt good, didn't it? (If you have never done something like this, you have other problems and need a different book.) There are hundreds of books out there on the art and science of gratitude, karma, and kindness. Check them out and start shifting your behaviors and actions into more loving, gracious, and kind ones.

One simple tool some people use to stop negative self-talk and be kind to others is to snap themselves with a rubber band or bracelet every time something bitchy comes out of their mouth. The stress-less bracelet is perfect for this and is a great reminder to breathe, relax, and, of course, to stress less. You can also try smiling more. Flipping that frown upside down is proven to boost your mood and the moods of those around you.

What Can I Do to Get Perspective?

Things really stink sometimes—for everyone. You are not the only person stressed out in today's world. Yet we manage to complain, compare, and fret over every negative situation that arises. If we can get over the constant negativity, we will be one step closer to a peaceful and less-stressed existence. There are many ways to get perspective on life, and what will work best will differ for everyone. Below are two ways to change your perception so that the big and small stressors of life seem less difficult. And don't forget about Life Mapping—the technique that is driving this whole process!

1. **Now, Then, Later Planning:** When we are faced with a tough decision, big life change, or giant stress, we often become so paralyzed by fear of what *might* happen that we get stuck. The big hairy monster of change scares us so much that instead of doing something—anything to get us closer to our next step—we stay where we are in a haze of anxiety. But if we can look at all possible scenarios of a change and look at both the positive and negative consequences that *might* happen, we can take away much of the fear and anxiety that causes us stress.

First imagine a big decision or change that is happening in your life that is holding you back from moving forward. Next imagine the outcome if you were to make the change or decision the way your heart really wants. Now imagine if you put the decision into action or you embrace the change today. How will your life feel right now? What will your relationships be like? How will you feel emotionally? What will your health be like? What will your finances look like? Now go longer term and think about how your life will be different, both positively and negatively, a year from now. And then go long, long term. In ten to fifteen years, how will your life be different, both positively and negatively, if you embrace a change or make a decision today?

If a decision or change won't impact you in any way, you are stressing out too much about it now. If it will impact you positively more than it will negatively, just go for it. If it will impact you negatively, then start brainstorming alternative actions to change the course of your life from being stuck to being able to move forward. By envisioning all of the good and bad consequences of a decision or life change, you take away much of the fear that causes the stress that paralyzes us.

2. **Integral Thinking:** Integral is a theory developed by Ken Wilber that ensures we are taking multiple perspectives into

account. There is much, much more to it than this brief exercise—so much so, in fact, that there is an entire master's program dedicated to integral theory. But very briefly, Integral can help you get out of your own head and look at how a stressor, change, or decision impacts not just your life, but the world around you as well.

In *Figure 1* (below), you can see that there are four quadrants to this way of thinking. The upper left is the "I" quadrant, which represents your inner feelings, thoughts, emotions, and characteristics of your personality. In the upper right is the "It" quadrant, which represents your external body, like your skin, organs, health, scent, and behaviors. In the lower left is the "We" quadrant, which is all about your relationships with others at home, work, spiritually, etc. In the lower right is the "Us" quadrant, which represents your place in the bigger world of systems, like environment, government, healthcare, etc.

Figure 1

I — **Internal thoughts, ideas, memories, feelings, etc.**	It — **External body, physicality, etc.**
We — **Your relationship with others, your social groups, your ethnic group, etc.**	Us — **Your connection to the universe, beyond your bubble, relationship with space and time, etc.**

You can look at your life through any or all of these lenses, and it will look different. The goal is to get them to all work in harmony. For me, I was always all about myself. I was grounded in my upper left quadrant and thought that my feelings and emotions were all that mattered. I didn't really care that much about the upper right quadrant, which is my health, aside from a bit of vanity about my appearance. I was more concerned about myself than any of the relationships in my lower left quadrant. And I certainly didn't have any feelings about my place in the bigger world. But after my daughter was born in 2006, my entire world shifted. Suddenly I was extremely concerned about relationships and my health. I needed my daughter to be fully embraced by me and needed to be around for a long time for her. After my husband died in 2007, my view shifted even more. I realized there is much more to my life than my little corner of the world. I have a clear impact on the lower right "bigger world" quadrant, and the things in this quadrant also impact me.

By using these quadrants to check in on myself periodically, I can be sure I'm focusing attention where it needs. If I don't get so sucked into my own little world, I won't forget about the other parts of life.

By seeing the positive and negative consequences of every situation and having a plan for dealing with them, we remove the fear that often stresses us more than necessary. You can take the above exercises and combine them or use just components of each, depending on your situation. They can be very powerful tactics to help you get control of the stress that takes us down sometimes. They can also help us move forward with an action plan instead of getting stuck in stress.

Now What?

Changing a lifetime of habits and self-sabotaging behaviors isn't easy, but with some simple steps, you can start to make changes quickly. It's all about making the choice to be positive and stop the victimizing habits before they spin out of control and take down everyone around you. If we can act as proactive directors of our own life's path, we will feel more in control, less fearful, happier, and less stressed. Try these action steps and you'll be one step closer to less stress in your life.

Secret #1 QUIT BITCHIN' Action Grid

Action Step	Guidelines	Time to Implement	Simple/ Medium/ Hard	Fun/ Easy/ Important
Make the Choice	Make the conscious choice to stop bitching, whining, complaining, nagging, and victimizing yourself. Just decide it's time to stop for the good of yourself and everyone around you.	Instant	S	I
Smile More	Stop frowning. Start smiling all the time.	Instant	S	FEI
Life Mapping	Take a week to really think about your Life Map and then get out some crayons or markers and create it.	1 day	M	FI
Gratitude Journaling	Write two to three sentences every day on what you are grateful for at that moment. Start today.	1 day	M	E
Stress "Snaps"	Every time you notice a negative comment or bitchy behavior, snap your Stress-Less bracelet. The goal is to snap less and less over time.	1 day	S	E
Be Honest	For one week, take note of any negative interactions you have—with whom and how they are resolved. Be honest with yourself about whether or not you are causing your own stress.	7 days	H	I
Social Media Positivity	For one week, only post positive stuff on your Facebook, Twitter, and other social media pages. If a friend posts something negative, only post a suggestion or solution for improvement. Keep the habit up once you see how good it feels.	7 days	M	EI
Find Solutions	When speaking with others about your problems, don't just complain. Actively seek out solutions.	14 days	M	I
Integral Map	Over the course of two weeks, notice where you spend your time and how you focus your energies. Map it out on the Integral Quadrants.	14 days	M	I
Now, Then, Later Planning	Take a current decision or change and go through the Now, Then, Later exercise. It takes practice for it to come naturally, so start doing this for big and small decisions on a regular basis to get used to thinking about positive and negative consequences.	30 days	M	I

Remember to use GOALS when deciding which ideas to try:

Gut-Checked: It feels right.

Obtainable: You can accomplish it in a reasonable amount of time with reasonable effort.

Actionable: You can take steps to making it happen right now.

Life-Oriented: It fits with your lifestyle right now. You have the support to make it happen.

Small Steps: The goal can be broken down into multiple, tiny steps.

Secret #2
Check, Check, ~~AAAANd~~ Check

The Art of Prioritizing, Organizing, and Productivity
(Even for the lazy, unmotivated, and
procrastinators out there like me!)

"The key is not to prioritize what's on your schedule,
but to schedule your priorities." —Stephen R. Covey

Resources:

Get downloadable worksheets and
tutorials for Secret #2
Check, Check, aaand Check at:

HHESecrets.com

Use your smartphone to scan the below
QR code to go there now.

Benefits:

- More in control of your time.
- Less stress over time crunches.
- More focus on important tasks.
- Less anxiety over unfinished projects and tasks.
- More time available for passions and hobbies.

What's on Tap?

As a consummate list maker, I always thought I was good at prioritization. But when I was thrust into single parenthood after my husband died unexpectedly, my lists became a must-have. I had lists for everything—baby supplies to buy, groceries to purchase, house projects to complete, bills to pay, work tasks to complete.... The lists went on and on. But despite all the lists, they weren't set up in a way that I knew what to do first. I had no idea what would have the most impact on my time, health, happiness, and stress levels.

Over time, I researched ways to be more productive. But how can we learn to stay on track when we have no system to even start on the right track? How can we make the right choices to know what we should focus on first when long to-do lists are a daily reality? The Happy Hour Effect Secret #2 outlines several approaches that can help us to take back control of our time and resources so we can live a less-stressed life. We will learn:

- Why we are so busy
- How to get organized
- How to get rid of half of your to-do list
- How to get kids involved
- Next steps

If your days feel like complete chaos with no structure or agenda, this chapter will help you refocus your energy and get organized to minimize stress and maximize life.

Why Are We So Busy?

Back in the day, life was pretty simple. Men went to work. Women took care of the house. The kids went to school and you would all spend a peaceful night at home doing chores and relaxing in front of the tube. Today, men and women work. Men and women share home duties. Kids are super-scheduled. And life moves a million miles an hour as we try to keep up with technology, friends, bills, and all the other responsibilities of everyday life. If you take a look at the list in **Figure 2**, you can see just a partial list of things we juggle every day at home. Add to that all of the work tasks in **Figure 3** that sneak up on us and pretty soon we're juggling more than we can handle. Something is bound to drop.

Figure 2	*Figure 3*
Home Responsibilities	**Work Responsibilities**
• Loss of a loved one	• New supervisor
• Birth of a child	• New employee
• Empathy/sympathy	• Promotion
• Job loss or change	• Possibility of layoffs
• Health problems	• Short staff and overwork due to
• Retirement	layoffs or leaves of absence
• Divorce/separation	• Restructuring
• New relationships	• New procedures
• Family difficulties	• Training requirements
• Overcommitted	• Customer/patient demands
• Spiritual practices	• Budgets
• Bills/money	• Schedule changes
• Holidays	• Pay cut or salary freeze
• Menopause	• Employee reviews
• Midlife crisis	• New facility
• New home/old home	• Public relations nightmare or bad
• New car/old car	press
• School	• Difficult coworker(s)
• Time for hobbies	• Lack of fulfillment or passion
• Needing "me-time"	• Hate your job
• Parenting	• And the list goes on...
• Caring for aging parents	
• And the list goes on...	

After a speaking gig at a health conference, I met a woman who was so overwhelmed by her to-do lists that she was seeing a therapist *and* on antianxiety medications—because of her schedule! She didn't feel equipped to handle all of the demands of her children's sports practices, her volunteer work, her home chores, and keeping up with errands and her job. She couldn't remember the last time she and her husband had been out on a date night or had even spent any time

Three Secrets to Getting Things Done with Power and Ease

by Heidi DeCoux, organizational and productivity expert

Once you have whittled your to-do list down to the important, high-impact items, it's time to get things done!

In my experience, there are three main secrets to getting things done with power and ease.

1. Pick three to five priorities each day

Before you close up shop for the day and head to bed, choose three to five high-priority items that you commit to completing the next day. By choosing five priorities or less, you are more likely to actually get them done, and you will have enough time and energy to do a good job on them. Imagine and get a clear picture of what you would accomplish this year if you got five, high-impact items done every day, six days a week.

2. Schedule your projects

When you take on a new project, outline the steps and estimate the time it will take for you to complete each step. Then schedule when you will complete each step. Put it in your calendar as if it's a meeting. It's a meeting with yourself to work on that project. This will ensure that you get the project done on time, and it will help prevent you from over-scheduling. If your calendar is a big, open canvas, it's easy to forget that you need to spend time on your commitments.

3. Be ergonomic with your schedule

Schedule your highly creative, intense projects during the times of the day that you are the most alert and energetic. For me, that's early in the morning. For you, it might be after lunch or late in the evening. By working with your body's rhythm, you will get more done with power and ease.

Heidi DeCoux is an organizing and productivity expert and founder of ClearSimpleLiving.com. You can get free access to on-demand workshops, checklists, and a home organization e-kit now at ClearSimpleLiving.com.

alone besides sleeping in the same bed. And she confirmed that sleeping is all they were doing. They had lost the spark, and she was burning out too. I hear stories like this all the time. There is just too much to do and not enough time to get it all done.

I asked the woman if she enjoyed doing everything on her list, and she looked at me and said, "Of course not, but I *have* to do them." We talked for a while about why she felt this way, and it all came down to a false sense of expectation. Other people expected her to be on the bake sale committee. Other people expected her to stay late at work. Other people expected her to have dinner on the table every night and a fully stocked cupboard at their disposal. After talking for a while she stopped, shook her head, and said, "Oh my God, I'm living a life that others want me to live, not my own life!" What a breakthrough—and she's not the only one who suffers from this type of overload and pressure.

Our to-do lists and schedules become a burden when they get filled up with tasks that others expect us to do—tasks that may be necessary but that don't fit with our view of a happy and healthy life. And pretty soon those tasks that others expect us to fulfill overflow our mental capacity for them. Pretty soon we are maxed out and burnt out. Pretty soon the therapist's chair and that bottle of pills seem like the only way to get our lives back under control. But those are only temporary bandages to the challenges we face when prioritizing our time and tasks. If we don't take steps to shift the balance from acting off the expectations of others to living for ourselves, we will always be living on a short fuse about to explode from the pressure we face.

How Can We Get Organized Fast?

We get so used to rushing and speeding from one to-do to the next, we often don't take a step back to really analyze what we are doing, why we are doing it, how we are doing it, and for whom we are doing it. With just a few minutes of thinking and some smart changes, we can shift our lives so we are more productive *and* so we have more time to do things we love instead of the daily grind and routine that causes us stress.

The first step is to really take a good and honest look at your to-do list. If you did the Life Mapping exercise at the beginning of the book, you should have a good grasp of everything you do on a daily, weekly, and monthly basis. If you didn't do the Life Mapping exercise, take some time now to write down every big and small task you do every day (week/month), including committees, carpools, errands, hobbies, classes, work tasks, etc. Now, as you look at this list, it's time to be honest and real about each item. For everything on the list, ask yourself these questions (some of them may seem silly, but really think about them):

- Why am I doing this task? Is it necessary to the survival, happiness, or health of me or my loved ones?
- What does this task entail? Are there ways I can make it easier?
- How much time does this task take? Could I find a way to make it faster?
- Who am I doing this task for? Can I enlist help or pass the task to someone else?
- Does this task make me happy or make me feel fulfilled?

These questions will start to guide you to a place where you better prioritize your lists, streamline your tasks, and even eliminate unnecessary stuff that just sucks your time and energy.

Can I Really Get Rid of Half of My To-Do List Today?

Take a look at your list again. If you are really honest with yourself, chances are you can either shorten, delegate, or eliminate the majority of tasks on your list. But guilt and a sense of responsibility to others cause us to keep doing things over and over, even when they aren't

Making Your Next Move Less Stressful

by Diane Keyes, home staging expert and author

Moving is one of life's most stressful events. Greater trauma—death, divorce, illness, job loss, or a financial setback—is often the reason for a move. Being prepared and organized reduces stress, decreases the time it takes to sell, and improves your chances for a profitable sale. And, almost without exception, the money you spend up front will be less than a price reduction if your home remains on the market.

Ten tips to *get you moving*:

1. Make a list of what needs to be done, focusing on clutter, cleanliness, and condition. A clean, uncluttered house in good condition will sell faster and for the best price every time.

2. Prioritize your list based on what items send a negative message to buyers. For several years we had a crack in the window visitors passed when coming to our door. Although the crack was not expensive to repair, we didn't fix it until we realized buyers would make damaging assumptions about the condition of our home.

3. Complete small projects first. It reduces stress by shrinking the list, giving you a feeling of control and accomplishment to carry you through the more time-consuming tasks.

4. Tackle items buyers will see first when they visit your home. Love is blind, and problems later in the tour are less of a concern when buyers are already "in love" with the house.

5. Do one task at a time. Most people who multitask aren't more productive—they just feel busier and more stressed, so they think they *must* be getting more done.

6. Handle things only once. When you pick something up, put it where it belongs. If you can't decide, put it out of sight in a box marked "undecided" so it's off your radar.

7. Make changes that are easy to live with. Don't take the leaves out of the table and move the chairs to the basement if you're having family for dinner this weekend. Most often, it's the combined effect of the changes you make that is important, not one killer idea.

8. Stick to your list. If you think of other things you'd like to do, put them on a separate list and consider them *only* after you've finished with your essential list.

9. Have a contingency plan for showings on short notice. No time to clean? Fill sinks with detergent for a few minutes to make the house smell fresh. Then pack up pets, throw dirty dishes into the oven or dishwasher, and use a couple of empty laundry baskets or storage bins to collect odds and ends.

10. If you don't feel you're ready to let go of your home but must move, throw a farewell party. Surround yourself with family and friends and share your memories of the good times you've spent there, asking for blessings on the new owners. These rites of passage help bring closure and will reassure you there are wonderful memories yet to come.

Whether decorating a four-star restaurant or the governor's mansion for royalty, or consulting on a $4.5 million island getaway or a two-bedroom bungalow, Diane Keyes is one of the country's premiere home stagers and the award-winning author of *This Sold House: Staging Your Home to Sell in Today's Market.* Find out more about Diane at thissoldhouse.biz and ifbhomesale.com.

useful (and they may even be hurting your situation). I want you to go through your list now, and using the questions above as a guide, make note of how you can change that task so it doesn't suck so much of your time and resources. Here is an example of common list items that I hear complaints about:

- **Go to grocery store:** I eliminated this task altogether by signing up for grocery delivery. The food doesn't cost any more than at the grocery store, the produce is hand selected by the packer, and the small delivery fee is well worth the time I save. And I actually save money because I only get what is on the list and don't get seduced by impulse buys. If you do only one thing on this list, this is the first one I recommend!

- **Make dinner:** This task is often near the top of the list of stressors people face every day. Set up a preplanned menu and include family favorites on the same night of the week: Taco Tuesday, Spaghetti Saturday, etc. Include your kids in the meal prep, and if they are old enough, assign them one night a week to prepare the meal. And always have your kids and significant other help with the cleanup. Cooking and cleaning will teach them responsibility, kitchen skills, and creativity. Combine the weekly meal planning with your grocery delivery and you'll kill two birds with one stone!

- **Clean closet/garage/shed/car:** These menial tasks are often on our lists but don't really need to be placed near the top unless they pose a safety hazard. Make these tasks a family affair and use the donate/dump/sell method for going through everything. Make piles of things to donate to charity. Bag them up and call the charity pickup right away so it doesn't clog up the house or garage. If it's a big job, rent a large dumpster or get an extra garbage can for the week and just throw everything right in. No need to sort it all out unless it's recyclable. Anything that can be sold, take a photograph and immediately post on

Craig's List or eBay. If you don't do it right away, it will go back on the shelf and keep collecting dust. If you haven't worn or used something in the last year, get rid of it. If you're cleaning a closet and the outfit doesn't make you feel confident and great, get rid of it. If an item hasn't fit you in over a year, get rid of it. Let go of emotional attachment to items, and remember that the memory of an item doesn't go away just because the item is no longer in your home.

- **Carpool/kids' sports/school committee/fundraisers:** These are tough ones because we feel we *must* do these things for our kids or because the school (and other parents) expects you to do them. This may be the case, but are there ways you can streamline the tasks? Do you really have to sell the most candy for your child's fundraiser? Or is it their responsibility to do it and not your job to solicit at work? Do you really have to make twelve dozen of the most complicated homemade cookie recipe you can find? Or would store-bought be okay? Do you have to show up and volunteer to be involved with every single project or committee meeting, or could you go quarterly and call it good? There are ways to decrease the time and energy you put forth on things that are important for others but not as important for you.

- **Work projects:** This one is a devil because you want to do a good job and get the job done quickly, but many of us have a hard time sharing credit or delegating tasks because we are perfectionists or it is just too much work to show someone else how to do something when we could just do it ourselves. Therein lies the problem. We are trying to control something that doesn't require us to be so involved.

- **Daily household chores:** The number one complaint I hear from people is that they wish they didn't have to spend so much time cleaning the house or picking up after the kids. I have a simple solution: hire a housekeeper. Unless you are extremely financially strapped, this can be the simplest and fastest way to relieve stress and find more free time. I have had a housekeeper for years. There are times I have her come every week or two and other times when money is tight that she comes once every month or two. It takes the pressure off of having to keep the house clean and gives me more time to spend with my daughter or doing hobbies. Many people shy away from a housekeeper because they are afraid of seeming snobby or don't want someone messing around in their home. But if you can get over these imaginary and silly worries and give it a shot, you will immediately realize how much they reduce your stress levels and lighten up your to-do lists. Hire one today!

You can see from the above examples that any task, no matter how important or how mundane, can be made easier or even be eliminated from your list if you just put in a little effort, forethought, and planning. Remember that a little work up front can save you countless hours of time in the long run.

How Can I Involve My Kids?

Note: If you don't have kids, you can still use the tips in this section as you learn to share tasks with roommates, family members, coworkers, or a significant other.

Kids love to be a part of things, and they need to learn how to live in the real world. If you do everything for them, they never learn responsibilities or even basic tasks like preparing a meal or cleaning the house. Never feel guilty for making your kids do chores or asking them to help with something. They need it, and so do you. It will benefit you both for the long term. You are the parent.

Believe me, I know how hard it is to negotiate with a kid. My five-year-old daughter is already a master manipulator, but as a widow mom, I can't let her have that kind of control over my time or emotions now or as she grows up. Kids need boundaries and rules, so use that to your advantage. Here are some ideas:

- **Start small.** This is extremely important, especially if your kids have been a bit spoiled or you've been a friend-parent and haven't enforced rules (it's okay—a lot of people are the same way). Don't thrust a huge chore list upon them. Give them one or two things to start with, like emptying the dishwasher or wiping down the bathroom countertops.

- **Use a chart.** This is especially helpful for young kids because they love to track their progress and "win" by completing all the tasks. I include things like eating fruits and vegetables, feeding the dog, cleaning her room, and emptying the dishwasher. Yes—even a five-year-old is fully capable of these types of chores.

- **Include easy tasks on the list.** Include things they already do, like brushing teeth, feeding the family pet, getting dressed, or taking out the garbage. Once they accomplish one thing and can check it off the list, they will be motivated to keep going (just like adults).

- **Get creative.** Maybe you've never considered asking your eight-year-old to do heavy labor in the house, but they might get a kick out of dressing up as a superhero and helping you haul junk to the curb. Think outside the box and make chores and to-do lists fun for your kids and for you.

- **Lower your expectations.** Don't expect your kid to be perfect. The key is to get them to help in even the smallest of ways. Over time, this will add up. I like to expect the worst and hope for the best with every project I give my daughter. That way, I am not holding her to unrealistic expectations or being too hard on her for a job that isn't done well.

- **Reward within reason.** If kids only agree to do something for a reward, it instills that behavior in them as they grow into adults—not a good trait. Instead, make the completion of the task itself the reward. For example, when my daughter helps me prepare meals, she knows her body is going to get super-duper strong from all that healthy food. That is her reward for making good food choices. When she feeds the dog, she knows she is helping the dog to be happy and healthy. That is the reward. Of course, a reward for a big task well done is always a great incentivizer! But try to avoid giving material rewards like toys and instead give rewards that are experience-based, like outings to the zoo, museum, theater, or concert.

Kids want to help. You just have to frame tasks in a way that appeals to them. No kid will respond to, "Tommy, go take out the garbage." But he might respond to, "Tommy, check out this gross rotten banana. I think it's starting to ooze. Can you take it outside and do something with it?" Silly example, but with kids, you must bring yourself down to their level of development. They haven't learned all of the wisdom and responsibilities that adults (well, most adults) have learned. It is up to us to teach them. In the process, we can use their learning to save us stress and headaches along the way.

Now What?

Everyone is plagued by to-do lists and responsibilities every single day. These tasks won't magically disappear on their own. But if you give your list some thought and take a little time to figure out easier and faster ways to do things, you may be surprised at how you are able to reduce or eliminate things that once sucked your energy and resources. Try these tips to start lightening your load and freeing up your time.

Lists for Less Stress

by Jacquie Ross, professional organizer
and certified life and family coach

It has become the new normal to feel overwhelmed with a never-ending to-do list. This is not a good thing. Life should be a happy balance of work and play, and feeling in control is an important part of it.

Having a schedule and routine in your personal life is as important as having one at work, yet many people don't know where to start. Here are some tips for feeling more organized and taking back control of your life with the help of your to-do list:

1. **Set goals.** What do you want your life to look like? What steps can you take to get there? For example, if you imagine yourself waking up to a clutter-free bedroom, an organized closet, and a neatly made bed, write down what you can do to accomplish this.

2. **Create a master to-do list.** Your master to-do list will list everything you need to accomplish, but it will be separate from your everyday to-do list. Use the master list as a "master plan," and review it weekly to see if you can tackle at least one task or project. Break down a larger project from your master list into smaller tasks, and then transfer each task to your everyday to-do list. By using a master list, your longer-term projects or goals won't get forgotten.

3. **Set priorities.** Once you have your goals and master to-do list written down, you can set your priorities. Using my example in number one, what would be the most important

goal to you? Would you start by decluttering your bedside table so that it only has the current book you're reading? Is your closet such a mess that choosing what to wear creates undue stress each morning? Prioritize your list and then work on one goal at a time.

4. **Find a list-making tool that works for *you*.** If you prefer to write things down on paper, then the next best app may not work for you. Don't force it. Use what works. If you want to try a new tool, then try it for about eight weeks. If it's not working, it probably never will. It takes about six weeks to learn a new habit, so if it didn't work, move on and try something else. It's not a failure—it just wasn't the right tool for you.

5. **Create daily and weekly routines.** If you struggle with the routines of daily life, e.g., cooking, cleaning, organizing, shopping, etc., create a weekly chore chart and do a little a day, or hire a service to help you. You may find that some tasks are simply worth hiring a service to do. Consider a manicurist or handyman. Just because you are able to do the job yourself doesn't mean you have to.

6. **Stop saying yes to everything.** Stop, think, and take a breath before responding to a request. Even better, tell the person you will get back to them. This will give you time to look at your schedule and responsibilities before making any commitments.

7. **Write everything down in your calendar.** At the end of the day, do you often find yourself saying, "What did I do all day?" We have a tendency to think that certain tasks don't take that long, so we don't properly schedule them. We then wonder why we're rushing around all the time. To avoid this feeling, it's a good idea to write down all of your tasks and chores in your calendar and treat them like an appointment.

No more wondering what you did all day, because much of it will have been clearly noted in your calendar.

8. **Turn down the noise.** If you struggle to stay focused, don't be afraid to turn off email and social media notifications. Schedule specific blocks of time to check email and social media. Timesaving technologies can also be time wasting if you're not careful to watch the time spent using them. By having specific blocks of time scheduled for these tasks, you will be more productive, more focused, and will get more done in less time.

9. **Get organized.** Yes. You've heard it all before, but getting organized really does improve your quality of life. If your home is cluttered and out of control, or if you struggle with managing your time, it may carry over into your work life, creating poor performance or missed opportunities at work. People who are organized are generally less stressed, more focused, and are more likely to reach their goals.

Taking control of your life is a step-by-step process that takes one day at a time. Taking control of your life also means scheduling time to do the things that matter most to you. So make time to create your master plan, and then take it from there. Over time, you will begin to see the positive results of your efforts as you create a more organized and less stressed life.

Jacquie Ross is a certified life and family coach, professional organizer, and the award-winning owner of CastAway the Clutter! Jacquie works with busy moms, families, and overworked professionals to develop strategies to clear their physical and mental clutter, reach their goals, and find more meaning in their lives. Learn more about Jacquie's organizing and life coaching services and get organizing tips in her declutter e-course at CastAwayTheClutter.com.

Secret #2 PRIORITIZATION Action Grid

Action Step	Guidelines	Time to Implement	Simple/ Medium/ Hard	Fun/ Easy/ Important
Get Grocery Delivery	This is the easiest and fastest way to eliminate an item on your to-do list. If you live in a community where this service is available, start today.	1 hour	S	E
Analyze Your Lists	Take a long, hard, honest look at your to-do lists and determine where you can simplify things.	1 day	M	I
Menu Planning	Every weekend, put together a menu plan for the week ahead and get your groceries ahead of time. Combine it with grocery delivery and you will kill two birds with one stone.	1 day	M	FE
Delegate to Others	Don't be a perfectionist or control freak. If someone else is capable, willing, and able to do a task, let them do it.	1 day	H	I
Eliminate Tasks	Many items are on our list simply because we feel we must do them for others or keep up with those around us. Be honest and let go of tasks that don't serve you.	7 days	M	I
Get a Housekeeper	If you can afford it, hire some help. Even if it's just a once-a-month deep clean, this service can be invaluable and free up hours and hours of time.	7 days	S	FE
Hire a Babysitter	Don't be ashamed or feel guilty about hiring a babysitter every now and then. You deserve and need time to recharge, and your kids need to learn to relate to other people.	7 days	S	EI
Let Go of Expectations	Don't do things because other people expect you to do them. Always know why you are doing something and whether it benefits you and your family.	14 days	H	I
Simplify	Don't overcomplicate tasks that can be simplified. For example, buying store-bought cookies is much easier than making several dozen homemade ones.	14 days	M	I
Involve Kids	Don't be a maid for your kids. Give them chores and get them to help.	21 days	S	FI

Remember to use GOALS when deciding which ideas to try:

Gut-Checked: It feels right.

Obtainable: You can accomplish it in a reasonable amount of time with reasonable effort.

Actionable: You can take steps to making it happen right now.

Life-Oriented: It fits with your lifestyle right now. You have the support to make it happen.

Small Steps: The goal can be broken down into multiple, tiny steps.

II.
Work

Resources:

Get downloadable worksheets and
tutorials for Secret #3
I Love My Job! at:

HHESecrets.com

*Use your smartphone to scan the below
QR code to go there now.*

Benefits:

- No more Monday blues.
- Weekends will be more enjoyable without work stress weighing on your mind.
- Relationships will become easier when you're not carrying the burdens of work all the time.
- You will be excited to go to work in the morning.
- You will have better relationships with your coworkers and superiors as you discover common goals.
- Your kids will see what it means to enjoy work and will learn positive behaviors.
- By embracing your passions and making them a part of your work life, you will never feel like you're at a job and will feel fulfilled by what you do every day.

Secret #3
I Love My Job
(sarcastic laugh)

How to Slay Stress and Do What You Love

"Everyone has been made for some particular work, and the desire for that work has been put in his (or her) heart." —Rumi

What's on Tap?

Raise your hand if you love your job. Anyone? Anyone? If you raised your hand, you are in the minority. If you didn't raise your hand, join the club. The sad truth is that while most of us spend the majority of our adult lives working, that huge chunk of time isn't the best or happiest it could be. Unless we've been bestowed a nice inheritance or trust fund, the economically-driven society in which we live requires us to work to pay the bills, feed our kids, take vacations, make our house payments, and, if we're lucky, have enough left over to retire on when our working days are done. And so we do it. We get up in the morning, punch the clock, come home, spend a few precious hours with our loved ones, go to bed, get up the next day, and do it again.

Most Americans say that their job is the top stressor in their lives. *The daily grind. Chained to a desk. Work prison. Boss from hell.* These aren't pretty descriptions of a place we have to spend so much time. And because our work takes up the majority of our time, we have it in our minds that we must have work/life balance—as if work is 50 percent and life is 50 percent, with each being completely separate. But they are so tightly enmeshed that a 50/50 split is ludicrous if not impossible. In fact, there are days that our energy and time actually overflow the confines of the twenty-four hours we have each day. We focus on work 50 percent of our day, we have a sick kid dominating our thoughts 90 percent of the day, we have a car repair sucking up 20 percent of the day, we have a health problem of our own monopolizing 100 percent of our brain power, and on and on. Pretty soon, our day isn't just 50 percent work and 50 percent life adding up to a neat and tidy 100 percent. Suddenly we're giving 2000+ percent of our time and energy as we constantly juggle and finesse all the moving pieces of our lives at any given moment. We are really just the conductors of an orchestra deciding what part of life rises to the top right now and what part will take precedence an hour or five years from now. It's a constant, moving, and dynamic dance we do every single second of every single day. No wonder we are stressed out keeping all those balls in the air!

And yet the fact remains that we spend the bulk of our time physically at work, butt in our chair, slaving away for the bulk of the day. So how can we make our working moments count? How can we spin our jobs and make them juicier, more exciting, and more meaningful? The Happy Hour Effect Secret #3 will open our eyes to a new way of working that is more fulfilling and less stressful. We will learn:

- Why jobs suck
- What we can do about a stressful boss or coworker
- How to change a job you hate into one you love
- Tips for reducing work stress
- How to find your passion and do what you love at work

Whether you're in corporate America, a construction worker, a healthcare employee, or an entrepreneur, work stress is inevitable. But with just a few small changes and a shift in your perspective, you can find energy and joy in your work while minimizing the stress that goes along with your job.

Why Do Jobs Suck?

Jobs can suck for so many reasons. And often times, just one small pain-in-the-butt task can make the rest of the job seem worse than it really is. Here are some of the big reasons why we find displeasure in our jobs:

- **Rewards**: Working our tails off for someone else's benefit isn't fun if we're not reaping some rewards too. They can be financial rewards like a paycheck, bonus, or commission. They can be spiritual rewards in that your job makes you feel connected to others or that you're making the world a better place. You may have ego rewards in the form of awards, recognition, or fame. Or you may have the reward of knowing you do a great job, work hard, and give it your all every day. When these rewards don't come, not only do we feel useless, but we feel taken advantage of and used. Our egos need the stroke whether we like to admit it or not.

- **Responsibilities**: Almost every worker has some part of their job that they dislike. Even those who adore their jobs have little annoyances that can turn a good day into a stressful one when that task comes up on the to-do list. For me, I cannot stand doing anything related to accounting or QuickBooks. Yet it's a necessary part of my job as a business owner. I absolutely love what I do every day, but when the time rolls around to get out the receipts, open that dreaded file on my computer, and start entering numbers, my shoulders tense up and my day goes south. When the job responsibilities that we dislike start to outweigh what we like about the job, that tipping point pushes us into stress zone.

- **Expectations:** This ties directly to the actual job description and what our bosses, clients, and coworkers expect from us in relation to that job description. Those of us who need clear-cut roles and responsibilities will suffer more angst when we're asked to work on new projects that don't fit our role. Those of us who are more resilient to change won't have a problem when we're asked to stretch our limits.

- **Schedule:** This is a sensitive subject. Some employers are firm believers in the 9-5 office culture with everyone at their desks in the same place at the same time, while others embrace flexibility and empower their employees to choose the best work environment for them. Neither culture is right or wrong, but if a company puts an employee who needs structure into a flexible work environment or hires a free spirit into a regimented culture, problems will arise.

- **Communication:** Everyone has their own preferred ways of communicating. I'm an email and text junkie who hates to talk on the phone. Some people prefer face-to-face communication. Others still prefer writing over speaking, or vice versa. No matter the preference, it is so important that all members of the team work together to understand everyone's communication style. Stress is inevitable if there is too much disconnect between a preferred style and a mandated style.

There are a million and one other reasons why a job might suck, but these are the big buckets that are catch-alls for most any reason a job might not measure up to what we expect. One of the most common challenges we face on the job is dealing with difficult coworkers. It is such a big issue that it deserves its own section. So read on to find out how to deal with that major job suck.

Does Your Job Stress You Out?

by Julie Bauke, career strategist and president of The Bauke Group

It's no big secret that our jobs consume the majority of our waking hours and are therefore often a source of significant stress. Before you can reduce that job stress, you have to identify the source of it. It is rarely the whole job that is the cause. To alleviate your job stress, you have to break it down. Here are some possibilities:

The work itself. It is possible that you are in the wrong job. I define the wrong job as one that does not utilize your true strengths and skills—one in which you feel like you are wearing size seven shoes on your size nine feet. As an example, if you are decidedly not a person who is good with detail, but your job requires that you spend all day mired in detail, you are in the wrong job.

The work environment or organization's culture. We all desire to belong to the right tribe, where we feel like we fit. If you feel like you have to mask who you are every day at work, this will certainly cause a great deal of conflict within yourself. If you are a thoughtful planner but your organization is filled with people who value quick action without much deliberation, then letting someone else clean up their messes, you probably spend your work days pulling your hair out.

The leadership. Of course, you don't have to idolize your manager or leadership team, but it does help to have respect for them and believe that they are leading in the right direction. If you're feeling out of sync with your leaders and the organization's direction, you will be stressed out, maybe even over the possibility of the loss of your job.

Your non-work life. Yes, sometimes the source of our stress is something unrelated to work, but we blame it on our job because it is an easy target. We have worked with many professionals who, upon serious reflection, are in a bad relationship, have family struggles, health issues, or any number of things that are the true source.

Once you have identified it, now what? Consider these tips:

Change your current situation in some way. Get very clear on what you have control over and what you don't. You undoubtedly have more control than you think you do. At the very least, you can change the way you think and act. Sometimes the smallest tweak to your situation can make a huge difference.

Add other activities to your life that balance you out. If you love being wildly creative but your job allows none of that, take a class or get involved in an endeavor that allows you to express your creative side.

Change jobs. Sometimes that is your only option. Before you begin any job search, you must know what you are looking for. If your only goal is to get away from your current situation, your likelihood of taking the wrong job again is very high. Identify what would make you "skip to the shower" on Monday mornings, and get as close to it as possible.

We all deserve to use our talents and skills not only for the greatest contribution at work, but in a way that makes us happy—or at the very least, not miserable.

Julie Bauke is a career strategist, president of The Bauke Group, and the author of *Stop Peeing on Your Shoes: Avoiding the 7 Mistakes That Screw Up Your Job Search*. Learn more at TheBaukeGroup.com.

I Hate My Boss (coworker, client, employee)! What Should I Do?

A bad boss, client, or coworker can make even your dream job a nightmare. When we are forced under someone's control who doesn't share the same beliefs, work ethic, culture, or communication style as we do, we are pushed out of our comfort zone, and stress sets in. Whether you have a bully for a boss, a credit-taking coworker, or you supervise a lazy slacker, it all goes back to motivation and understanding.

How may times have you wished bad tidings on the offender? Be honest. We've all imagined the demise of that nightmare boss, stopping just short of making it a reality like the ladies did in the movie *9 to 5* or like the guys did in the movie *Horrible Bosses* (both highly recommended if you haven't seen them). I had a former boss I referred to as "the devil in hockey gear," and another I called "Satan." Notice a theme there? I was blaming these people for every evil and bad thing happening in my life at those times. But in hindsight, I thank them both every single day because if it hadn't been for their behavior pushing me out of my comfort zone and into borderline psycho zone, I would never be where I am today as a stress management guru, doing what I truly love to do every single day. But how do you get to that place?

1. The first step is to **find common ground** with that pain-in-the-butt person at work who tests your criminal mind. Are they having tough times at home? Do they have goals they are being pushed to hit that you aren't aware of? Do they have a big ego that needs major stroking? Do they need recognition? Do they understand *your* needs and motivations? That is a lot of questions with a million different answers, but the point is that we all have personality traits, health issues, relationship challenges, emotional needs, etc. that drive our behaviors both at home and at work. Unfortunately, when we don't take the time to understand and really know a person, we may

never get to know the person who is underneath all of the negative stuff that is on the surface. When you get sucked into stress because of the annoying coworker, ask yourself these questions and try to empathize. They may be having a bad day (or a bad life). And remember that you may have been an offender at one point or another too. It's a two-way street, so try to cross over sometimes and see the other person's point of view.

2. The next step is to **communicate better**. Perhaps you are only hearing what you want to hear and aren't really listening. Or you are asking or telling in words but not saying it clearly so the person understands it. There are thousands of books on communication, so I won't go into the nitty gritty, but just remember that there are filters we all have when we listen and speak. Learn to be clear, detailed, and to the point, and ask for clarification when you don't understand something. The more you can find shared understanding, the easier it will be as a project or relationship progresses. And give the bad guy the benefit of the doubt. For their sake, let's hope they aren't intentionally being a jerk.

3. Finally, **change your reaction** to this person's behavior. If they are out looking for a pat on the back, give it to them and move on instead of getting yourself worked up about it. If they are a micromanager, continue to show them you are a skilled and effective worker. Develop some easy reports you can feed to them regularly so they are "in the know" but stay out of your hair. Find ways to make the difficult person happy and you will be happier in return.

Don't get me wrong: a bad boss or coworker *can* be the devil in disguise. They can make life a living hell for you at work and at home. But if you can change your reaction, make the other parts of your life more enjoyable, and do work that makes you feel fulfilled and connected, their drama will become less stressful for you over time.

How Can I Turn a Job I Hate into One I Love?

If you are stuck in a tough job situation with no way out, it can make the already big stress of the job itself even more scary and unmanageable knowing you're stuck. When I was newly widowed, I was stuck in a truly awful job situation, but as a mom of an infant, I was terrified to leave the job because I needed the health insurance and security of a regular paycheck. And I did suffer through it for two years before I discovered the secrets to less stress and made the change I knew I needed to make. I left my safe and secure corporate America job and took a leap of faith to start my own company, and thus, Happy Hour Effect was born! And I haven't regretted it a day in my life. I've had times I have been so poor I wasn't sure how I would pay my bills the next month, but the universe has always come through for me. But if there is ever a day when it doesn't, I know the worst that could happen is that my daughter and I will be living in my parents' basement while I figure it out.

When I look back on my time at difficult jobs, some key coping mechanisms jump out—ones that made the most unbearable situations not so bad. They may not all work for you, but try them and see which ones work best for your particular scenario.

- **Ask for new responsibilities.** When you are bored, burnt out, or just plain over your job, the best first step is to try and get something new on your plate. Even just a simple task done once a week can breathe new life into a stagnant job. Look at your company and its products or services and pinpoint some of them that excite you. Try to find something in that area you could do to benefit the company. Remember to always make it about the company, not about you (even though it really is about you and your happiness). Position the request to your boss in a way that doesn't cut into your current responsibilities. Over time, make it a bigger and bigger part of your job and slowly minimize others as you show the value that the new task has for the company. This one isn't an overnight solution, but over time can do wonders for your stress levels.

- **Seek out allies.** When work stress takes you down, find friends at work whom you can talk to about it. If you try to suffer through it on your own without finding a solution, it will just get worse and worse. The key is to not just seek out the allies but to work together to come up with real ways you could make the situation better. Don't just have bitch sessions.

- **Get out of the office.** Sometimes a change of scenery is all you need to become reenergized. If your company offers services or products, suggest to your boss that you go out in the field for some competitive or consumer research. If there are relevant tradeshows, seminars, or events you can attend, explain how your attendance will benefit the company. Any new point of view can change your perspective and get you thinking differently about your job and your company.

- **Remember that management isn't the enemy.** Bosses, executives, and CEOs all have big responsibilities. Not only do they have to manage the work of their subordinates, but they are responsible for the overall direction and success of the company. They have big budgets, short and long term goals, and employee morale to deal with at any given time. They aren't out to get you, but if your performance or something within your realm of responsibility is falling short of meeting the big corporate goals, they may have no other choice than to come down a little hard to get things back on track. When things feel tense or you question decisions being made, remember that there are bigger goals and plans of which you aren't a part.

- **Avoid comfort foods at work.** When we are stressed out, our bodies are flooded with chemicals that prompt the fight or flight reaction. Cortisol, adrenaline, and a host of others circulate throughout our bodies and do damage in the process if we don't take action to counteract them. When we are stressed we are also tempted to seek out comforting activities, including food. We want something that makes us feel good again, so we reach for the soda or bag of Doritos for a temporary fix. If you look at the ingredients on these types of foods, you will find a list of chemicals and man-made ingredients. These chemicals get in your body and mix with those stress chemicals, and your body turns into a big, circulating vat of toxic sludge. Instead, opt for healthy foods and beverages when you're stressed. Fruits and veggies, nuts, tea, and coffee are much better choices because they actually contain antioxidants that can counteract and protect you from the damage caused by stress chemicals.

- **Remember it's business—not personal.** So many of us take a work criticism personally. We assume that a negative comment on a report or project means that we are bad people. But if you can learn to separate yourself from the business-related criticisms and remember that they don't make you a bad person, you will feel much less stress when negative comments come along. Instead of fretting and stressing when negative situations arise, try to spin it into a positive challenge of how you can do better next time.

- **Leave work at the office.** Most of us have come home from a bad day at work and let it ruin the rest of our night or weekend. In fact, not only have we let it ruin our own time at home, but we've complained and bitched so much that it has actually made our loved ones feel stressed and negative, too, because we just can't let it go. We've sucked them into our web of stress without even meaning to, just by bringing work home with us. Next time you have a bad day, leave it at the office. If you need to do a quick mention when you get home and let your family know you need fifteen minutes to decompress, do it. But then let it go. It's not worth it to destroy a night of fun and relaxation for yourself, and you certainly don't want to wreck someone else's time either. Leave your work stress at work!

• **Remember that change is inevitable and an opportunity for growth**. If you worked for a company that never changed, it would probably be out of business and you would be out of a job. Only those companies that flex, grow, and change will make it in today's world. Yet many employees are so afraid of change that they actually cause companies to struggle and even go under when a change isn't embraced. If you're one of those naysayers who always questions new policies or puts down any new idea, get your head out of your rear and look at the big picture. Change is good for the company in relation to what is happening in the market and amongst its competitors. Remember that management isn't the enemy and their goal isn't to drive the company into the ground with the changes they are making. And heck, there might even be some cool, new opportunities for you as part of the change. Remember when we talked about seeking out new responsibilities to make your job more interesting? Here's a perfect time to ask! Embrace change and learn to love it.

I'm Ready for a Big Change! How Can I Find My Passion to Do What I Love?

Changing careers or starting your own business can be very scary. But if you are ready to change your perspective and discover a new career path, there are many ways to do it without leaving behind the security of a regular paycheck until you're ready to take the leap. Here are just a few suggestions to get you started on the right path:

Tips for Managing Stress at Work

by Tai Goodwin, coach, speaker, and blogger

Long hours, overwork, burnout, long commutes, dysfunctional co-workers, micromanaging boss, underappreciated, deadlines, long meetings, never-ending email...we could go on and on and on with causes of work-related stress. While there are hopefully times when the fog lifts and work feels and truly is enjoyable, we all have those periods where the stress gets overwhelming.

When it comes to dealing with work-related stress, there are many options—some good, some not so good. Some people use food, while some turn to drinking too much or other destructive options that might alleviate stress for a short period. But the best options are positive approaches that take away stress and add well-being.

Physical Ways to Treat Job Stress

When you want to manage being overwhelmed and stressed at work, try these activities:

1. Hit the gym either before or after your workday.
2. Find a place to take a fifteen-minute power nap.
3. Go for a walk on your lunch hour.
4. Squeeze a stress ball to give yourself something to focus on.
5. Take a few slow, deep breaths whenever you feel stressed to relax your muscles and bring more clarity.
6. Monitor what you eat and drink. Too much sugar and caffeine can have a negative impact.

Mental Ways to Handle Job Stress

You don't always have to do something physical in order to let go of stress. Mental and emotional options can work too. Consider these mental stress relievers:

1. Read a lighthearted and enjoyable book.
2. Start a journal—get everything out of your head and onto paper.
3. Watch a movie that makes you smile and laugh.
4. Talk with a loved one about a happy time you shared. Reminiscing can be very good for you.
5. Pray or meditate about your concerns and how to deal with them.
6. Recite positive affirmations to yourself each day, before and after work.

Remember, what works for you to alleviate stress might be different than what works for someone else. Experiment with different options to find what works best for you. Practice with more than one technique so you always have a variety of stress-relieving choices that can fit any situation or environment. Once you find what works, you can use it regularly to keep your job stress to a manageable level.

Does your career need a makeover? Tai Goodwin is a speaker, coach, and blogger on a mission to help professionals create careers they can love and live with. Visit careermakeoverocoach.com for articles and tips for making work "work."

1. **Find your passion.** This is often easier said than done, but usually, a passion is that thing you can do for hours and hours, yet it seems like only moments have passed. For me, I have three or four things like this. One of them happens to be writing. I can write for hours and hours, and suddenly an entire day has gone by. Another one is gardening. I can be out in the yard putzing around for an entire weekend, and it goes by in an instant. Those kinds of activities are where you should put your focus. If you aren't sure where your passions lie, there are many great books and tools out there to help guide you, but most of us know instinctively what we love to do.

2. **Don't quit your day job—*yet.*** Until you are sure you are truly passionate about what you think you're passionate about, it's best to stick with your steady paycheck while you explore your options. When I left my corporate America job to start Happy Hour Effect and write my first book, it wasn't on a whim. I had a plan in place and had been researching and taking small steps for over a year. If you can simultaneously save some extra money to fund your new venture, even better.

3. **Start small.** Don't think that if you decide to open a scrapbooking shop, it will happen overnight. Even someone who dreams of being a writer can't just sit down and crank out a book overnight when all they need is paper and pen—or nowadays, a laptop. Most dreams and goals require time, planning, and usually some money. Sit down and map out all of the small steps you can take along the way, and start working on them, but don't focus so much on the end result or you will get overwhelmed. (See the section on GOALS at the beginning of the book for more on this.)

4. **Find your people.** Going it alone can be frustrating and lonely. Find others who share your passion. Join networking groups, clubs, and associations. Attend any events pertinent

to your passion and network like crazy. I'm a total introvert and completely uncomfortable in social situations like this, but I force myself to do it because I know it will help me realize my dreams faster than if I muddle through alone.

5. **Do one new thing every day.** Research your dream goal on the Internet. Start a notebook or journal to keep track of your ideas. Go to the library. Do some market research. Whatever you do, you need to commit to your dream and make it a real part of your life now so you can learn to live and breathe with it. Keep it on your to-do list and you will get closer and closer to reaching the end goal.

6. **Take classes.** Learn every detail of your new opportunity or passion. If you love to draw and dream of being a comic book artist, take as many classes as you can on art, design, and writing. Community education and online classes can be very affordable or even free. You just need to seek them out. And you will not only meet great people to network with who share your passions, but you will gain credibility by having the education behind you.

7. **Write, blog, chat.** Do this for fun, not pay. If you can't commit yourself to spending time every day or every week writing or chatting about your dream industry, product, or job for free, then you aren't passionate enough about it to do it (or yourself) justice by pursuing it as a career. A true passion is something you can't imagine *not* doing, regardless of the money you get out of it. I write because it fuels me. I would do it even if I didn't or couldn't sell books.

8. **Become an expert.** All of the above steps really culminate into you becoming an expert on your topic, job, product, etc. The more you know the more confident you will be in going after your dreams. You won't have the fear of failure holding

you back, because you will be educated and know every in and out of your passion.

9. **Change your view on money.** Once you can separate money, security, passion, and work into separate buckets, you will have made a huge stride forward in following your passion. Most people think that changing jobs, starting a business, or following a dream requires boatloads of money. Sometimes it does, but most of the time it doesn't. When I was considering leaving corporate America, I had it in my head that the cost of health insurance for me and my infant daughter would make it impossible to leave—but I was wrong. Once I did the research and found the right solution, I was amazed at how little it would actually cost me to be self-insured. So start to change your view on money and shift your relationship to it. I'm not saying it isn't important. In fact, it is, and it's a requirement that you have some flow of income or savings to survive in today's world. But if you look at your situation, develop realistic budgets, and understand that you actually need less, you may be surprised. I have had years when I have made six figures in corporate America and years when I have had negative earnings owning my own business. The years I've made less have been the years I've been the most happy. You can discover this too once you stop tying money to happiness. (See the Money secret for more.)

As you begin to build your confidence and knowledge around your passion, you will feel it pulling at you more and more. As that happens, your brain will naturally begin formulating plans and ideas to make it a real and meaningful part of your life. So go after it, start immersing yourself in it, and enjoy it! In the short term, the energy it gives you will balance out the stress of your everyday stresses. In the long term, it just might become a career that will drive you to something big and great!

Now What?

Work stress can be the most debilitating kind because it takes up so much of our time. Not only do we physically spend the bulk of our time there, but we carry the stress home with us, and it seeps into our relationships and even affects our health if we don't manage it properly. But there is hope for making a crappy job situation more pleasant—heck, even enjoyable. Try these action steps we discussed throughout the chapter and you'll be one step closer to working at a job you love.

Secret #3 WORK Action Grid				
Action Step	Guidelines	Time to Implement	Simple/ Medium/ Hard	Fun/ Easy/ Important
Avoid Comfort Foods	Stress chemicals make your body toxic. Adding processed junk food and soda only adds to that toxic environment, so go fresh and healthy at work.	1 day	S	EI
Management isn't the Enemy	Bosses and executives have pressures and goals that may not be part of your world at work. Remember that they aren't intentionally being a jerk (or at least we hope not). They may have to take unpleasant actions to reach the bigger goals.	1 day	M	I
Leave Work at the Office	Instead of ruining your happy time at home with your loved ones with complaints about work, leave it at the office. Take fifteen minutes when you get home to decompress, and then let it go.	1 day	M	FI
Do One New Thing Daily	Every single day do something that either gets you closer to your dream or boosts your knowledge of your industry or expertise.	1 day	S	FE
Change Your Reaction	Instead of getting worked up the next time you're annoyed at work, let it roll off your back. Discover what the offensive person needs, and give it to them.	1 day	H	I
Start Small	Break a giant goal into smaller steps so it's easier to make progress and stay motivated.	1 day	S	EI
Write, Blog, Chat	Spend time sharing your insights and thoughts on your passion. If you can do this without pay, it is a good path.	1 day	S	F
Communicate Better	Be clear in your communication and ask for clarification if you're unsure of what to do next. Make sure you communicate with others in a way that works for both of you (email, phone, etc.). The best way to learn that is to just ask them.	7 days	M	I
Ask for New Responsibilities	When work gets boring or awful, ask for new responsibilities in an area that energizes you. What boss wouldn't be thrilled by a proactive employee? They will be happy, and you will reengage with your job in a positive way.	7 days	S	FE
Seek Cut Allies	Don't suffer work stress alone. Chances are someone else at the office is feeling the same pressures as you. Find a work friend and work together to find a solution to the problem.	7 days	M	F
It's Business, Not Personal	A negative criticism at work doesn't mean you're a bad person. It is an opportunity to improve for next time. Don't take work negatively to heart.	7 days	M	I
Find Common Ground	Learn to empathize and see things from your boss or coworker's point of view. It's a two-way street.	14 days	M	I
Find Your Passion	When you work on an activity or hobby that makes time fly by, that is your passion. If you're not sure what it is, get to the library and find a book to help you discover yours. Then start to do more of it.	14 days	H	FI
Find Your People	Go to networking groups, classes, tradeshows, and events where people in your dream industry or job hang out. Meet people and learn the ropes.	14 days	S	FE
Get Out of the Office	A change of scenery can do wonders for work stress. Go to a tradeshow or seminar. Take a class. Do some research via store or competitor shopping trips. Bring back new insights for the company so you can keep getting out.	14 days	S	F
Take Classes	Always be learning and boosting your credibility as an expert in your field. It will increase your confidence and keep you motivated too.	14 days	S	F
Don't Quit Your Day Job—YET	As you work on a big change or goal, stick with the security of a paycheck while you figure out your plan. Don't jump ship right away.	30 days	S	I
Become an Expert	Always add to your skill set to become a true expert on your passion. The more you know, the easier it will be to move ahead with confidence.	30 days	M	FI
Change Your View of Money	Begin to separate your definition of money from your definition of success. Make a realistic budget. Scrutinize your spending. Cut out nonessentials. You may be surprised how little you actually need to turn a passion into a career.	30 days	H	I
Change is Inevitable	Any company that doesn't change will fail. Companies that change are flexing with the trends, so go with it and use it as an opportunity for your own growth and development.	30 days	H	I

Remember to use GOALS when deciding which ideas to try:
Gut-Checked: It feels right.
Obtainable: You can accomplish it in a reasonable amount of time with reasonable effort.
Actionable: You can take steps to making it happen right now.
Life-Oriented: It fits with your lifestyle right now. You have the support to make it happen.
Small Steps: The goal can be broken down into multiple, tiny steps.

Secret #4
Money, Money, Money

Why More Green Doesn't Equal More Happiness

"Life is short and so is money." —Bertolt Brecht

Resources:
Get downloadable worksheets and
tutorials for Secret #4
Money at:

HHESecrets.com

*Use your smartphone to scan the below
QR code to go there now.*

Benefits:
- More control over your finances.
- Less dependence on money for happiness.
- More enjoyment of nonmaterial experiences and purchases.
- Less anxiety when bills arrive.
- Fewer arguments over money.
- Pay off debt quicker.
- Teach kids positive money habits.

What's on Tap?

Oh the elusive dream to be a millionaire with no worries, unlimited opportunities, and endless happiness. Because that's what it would be like, right? All of our problems would magically disappear and we would be stress-free. Right? If only that were the case and money could truly buy happiness. But as research has shown time and time again (and as the lottery winners of the past have proven), money isn't the cure to our woes. In fact, the old saying that money is the root of all evil may have more merit than we ever thought.

Now I'm no money expert. In fact, with my smattered financial history, I have no business doling out money advice. I have maxed out credit cards. I've saved massive amounts of money and then blown it. I have had years with negative income and years with six-figure income. I'm certainly no money maven. But what I have come to realize is that despite my money ups and downs, I haven't let it affect my outlook on life. Of course I have been nervous when money has been tight. And of course I have worried about my daughter's well-being. But I have always paid the bills and always put food on the table, and that is really all I've needed. Debt hasn't bothered me, while riches haven't added to my happiness. And in reality, the years I have reported six figures on my taxes have been my unhappiest years, while the years I've been in the hole have been amazing.

While I have developed this unique financial outlook, money still remains at the top of the list as a main stressor in most people's lives. How can we change our relationship to our finances and money so it's not one of reliance or negativity, but one of freedom and positivity? The Happy Hour Effect Secret #4 will reveal several ways to view money differently so it energizes instead of stresses us. We will learn about:

- The truth behind money and happiness
- Why money matters
- How to change our money mindset
- Next steps

If you find yourself worrying about bills, or if you define your success and happiness by how much money you have, this chapter can help you reframe your relationship with your finances.

MoNey vs. HappiNess

The goal of this chapter (and of life) is to help you feel happiness and peace—regardless of your bank balance. But in reality, no matter what I say or what you have learned up to this point, our relationship with money has been with us since an early age. We saw how our parents lived, and that formed how we live. We saw how they handled money, and that has influenced our financial habits in both good and bad ways. I met a man at a conference who told me that even though he and his wife make plenty of money, with their retirement all set, they still fight all the time about their finances. He had been raised with very poor parents, and he is a very frugal saver. His wife had also grown up poor, but she was affected in the opposite way. Since she had never been able to spend freely, she now feels it is her right to be able to spend the money they make on anything and everything she wants, from vacations to shoes to cars. This difference in mindset about money had been slowly driving them apart over the years, and they were on the verge of divorce, despite the security of their financial situation. She was defining her present happiness based on what she could buy. He was defining his present happiness based on his ability to secure his future. Neither is wrong. They are just different, and they couldn't find common ground upon which to approach their finances.

On the opposite end of the spectrum as the couple above, I met a woman who was about to lose her home. She had lost her job, and her husband was on disability. They had three kids from ages six to fourteen to feed, clothe, and put through school. After a few months of scraping by, they couldn't make their house payment, and it went into foreclosure. Yet despite these grim circumstances and the fear of the unknown, the couple was as happy and in love as ever. They still spent time together. They enjoyed a great sex life. Their kids were well-adjusted. They found ways to have fun on a shoestring. Somehow, they had found a way to rise above the stress of their financial situation to continue living a life of love and happiness, even though they were on the brink of financial ruin.

Whenever I recall these two very different scenarios, it gets me thinking about this definition of happiness and success that we all hold in our minds. Life can be amazing and wonderful, yet we let a financial setback or difference hold us back from true happiness. Or we can be bankrupt or have immense debt yet still look at the world through rose-colored glasses, not letting the void in our wallets prevent us from finding joy in our daily lives.

There is a vast amount of research that shows that money alone can't buy happiness. Having enough and having a lot don't cause major differences in levels of happiness. Those who are well-off can and do experience the same stresses and setbacks as those who aren't as financially secure. How can we tap into our own inner joy so that money isn't our definition of success and happiness?

Change Your Money Mindset

Everyone has a unique relationship with money. Some are driven by it. Others can do without and be perfectly content. Others still feel the need to save, save, save for the future while putting off present expenditures. No matter what your money mindset, you can shift it so you are finding happiness and enjoyment from life that isn't defined by how much money you have (or don't have). Here are some ways to stress less about money so you can be happier and less fearful about your financial situation:

- **Stop victimizing yourself.** Many of us are thrust into negative financial situations that feel beyond our control. We may have been laid off in the down economy. A partner may have overspent, leaving you with debt. Student loans may take up a huge chunk of your budget. Whatever it is, we often feel like victims and act out that victim mentality by having a woe-is-me attitude instead of taking responsibility and making changes to improve the situation. Go back and review Secret #1 to help shift this mindset.

- **Be grateful.** Every day, write down three things you are thankful for in your life. This daily practice will naturally shift your thinking over time from money-focused thoughts to more positive ones.

- **Set a budget.** When our finances spiral out of control, stress sets in. By taking a long, hard, honest look at your financial situation and setting up a plan to get back on track, you will feel more in control and less anxiety about money.

- **Be honest with your partner (and with yourself).** If you share finances with a spouse or significant other, you *must* communicate openly about your money. Hiding debt or having a secret account will only add to your stress and guilt. Get everything out on the table and set up your budget to fit the whole picture, not just one or the other in the relationship.

- **Don't place blame.** When hard financial times hit, it's easy to point the finger at someone else for why it's happening. Even if someone else is at fault, shift your language so you take responsibility together for how to make changes.

- **Pay with cash.** Every financial book I have read reinforces this rule. I can tell you that I do not follow it, but I should. It prevents overspending and the use of credit cards. You can directly see how much you are spending and feel more of a connection to the money than when paying with plastic.

- **Don't use retail therapy as a reward.** I am guilty of this all the time. Something good happens or I need to feel better and I hit

The Emotion Behind Money

by Julie Murphy Casserly, financial expert and author

Our emotions directly affect our money—how we spend it, why we spend, and when we spend it. And a big indicator for when we have an emotional spending spree is how stressed we are at the time. When we feel stressed, our bodies pump out stress hormones that affect us physically, mentally, and emotionally. Our heart rates speed up. Our muscles become tense. We breathe faster. And blood rushes to our brains, drastically altering the way we think and feel. As our bodies go into "fight or flight" mode, we are more likely to make financial decisions that we could very well regret in the future. Instead of dealing with the issue at hand, we use money to feel better. Unfortunately, the good feelings we get from spending it subside quickly once we check our bank accounts.

How do we get out of this pattern? We plan for it. Managing your money doesn't have to be stressful. In fact, it can be a great source of stability in your life if you know exactly what you have and how to govern it. Having a financial plan in place eliminates the fear of not knowing if you can afford something. Being fully aware of your current financial situation—all of your debts, your savings, your available cash, and your retirement fund—is the first step in regaining control over your money. Sitting down and going through all of your finances may be intimidating or even scary, but not knowing where you are financially will only create more stress in your life.

Let go of the stress surrounding your financial situation. Stop blaming yourself for the debts you have. Instead, sit down and calculate exactly how much money you owe and dedicate a reasonable portion of your monthly income to paying it down. Ignore the feeling of shame associated with having created that debt and replace it with a feeling of empowerment. Be proud that you're taking meaningful steps toward getting rid of it. Stop judging yourself and stacking up your finances to those of your friends and family, for this only fuels the stress instead of quelling it. Feeling guilty about what you did in your past is the cause of the stress you feel now. Let go of all of these negative feelings associated with money and you'll have a stress-free, as well as healthy, relationship with it from now on.

Julie Murphy Casserly is a sixteen-year veteran of the financial services industry and founder of JMC Wealth Management. She is also the author of the book *The Emotion Behind Money: Building Wealth from the Inside Out*, and she has been featured in media across the country. Julie's mission is to "financially heal the world" by helping people understand their emotions behind money and how these attitudes affect how they earn, spend, and save—or, conversely, accumulate debt. Uncover more at: JulieMurphyCasserly.com the mall. Or my daughter needs an incentive to do something, so I bribe her with a toy. Not a good plan. Instead, give yourself a home pedicure, go out for a date night, or spend a night out with friends. You will feel more satisfied and happier with the purchase of an experience than with a material one.

- **Consolidate your debt.** The simpler and easier it is to track your finances, the more motivated you will be to stay on track. Combine accounts, consolidate debt, and keep it simple.

- **Have a goal.** Putting a bigger financial goal in place to work toward can help you stay on track. Start a savings account or even a piggy bank to save for a vacation, house down payment (I recommend the bank for this), or even something as simple as a special night out with your significant other.

- **Eliminate nonessentials.** Video membership: $8/month. Movie channel on cable: $10/month. Newspaper subscription: $10/month. Fancy dog bones/treats: $40/month. (Yep—my expenses!) That is almost $70/month right there on things that I don't really need! Paying an extra $70 on a credit card or putting it into savings will be much more beneficial, and you won't even notice the things are gone. Replace the services with other things, like outdoor activities. Replace the fancy dog treats with homemade ones (cheaper and healthier for the dog). Analyze your budget and start cutting these trivial expenses out right away.

Just a few small tweaks to your financial plans can make a huge difference in how you feel and interact with others. The key is to be honest with yourself, honest with your loved ones, and to make decisions that benefit you instead of hurt you. Once you can get to a place of sharing a money mindset that serves you and your loved ones well, your stress will subside and you will feel less reliant on money as a definition of your success and happiness.

Now What?

Take an hour this weekend to really analyze your financial picture. Start to draft a plan that will help you feel more in control of your expenses and help maximize where your income is going. Over time, you will begin to release the hold that money has over your mindset and get to a place where you define your happiness based on life experiences and not the money that buys them. In a nutshell, the ideas just discussed in this chapter will help you get started.

Six Tips to Get Money Confident

by Ornella Grosz, personal finance expert, author, and speaker

More than ever we realize we have only ourselves to depend on for our financial success. Your brain can be your worst enemy, easily manipulated, and, typically, irrational. Listening and engaging in constant financial negativity (which you can't control) doesn't reduce your financial worries. But here's something you should know: envisioning decades ahead doesn't always come naturally to us. Therefore, you might struggle with your finances. It's not always your fault! The human brain is built for survival. It shouldn't be a surprise that many people struggle with investing, budgeting, and saving. Money concepts have to be taught. Implementing some of my tips will help you increase your confidence and make better financial decisions. Don't be so hard on yourself. To remove the emotions that seem to pair up with your financial decisions or lack of them, treat your personal finances like a business.

Here are six tips to increase your confidence with *your* money:

1. **Get financially naked.** Treat your finances like a business. Expose yourself to your financial truths. When it comes to money, we refuse, shy away from, or procrastinate taking a really detailed look at where our money is going and where it's not going. I understand the emotions that will be evoked from this financial exposure, but you have to get real with yourself. You can't move forward or increase your confidence if you don't know where you stand. Reviewing all your financial accounts, such as bank accounts, retirement accounts, and debt, will provide you with a reality check of your financial circumstances.

2. **Follow your money.** This is the opposite of creating a budget. For one month, write in a money diary how you spend your money. The amount of money you spend is not as important as the reason *why* you spent your money. Tracking all your *whys* will provide you with insights to your spending habits. Once you understand the reasoning behind your decisions, evaluate the amount of money spent and see where you can reduce your expenditures.

3. **Organize your financial life.** Come up with a system to manage and review your financial accounts in one snapshot. For instance, you can use Mint.com or an Excel spreadsheet to manage your finances. In addition, have a file system where you store important documents, such as insurance policies, tax records, retirement and investment statements, debt statements, home repair/maintenance, etc. Whether you use a plastic file container, scan all documents into your computer, or a combination of both, streamlining your financial documents will make your life easier.

4. **Get out of credit card debt.** There is absolutely no way you can build wealth by slaving your money to debt. Interest accruing on credit card debt binds you to a longer payoff period, and you will pay more for your original purchases. Regardless of how you ended up in this debt, please do not sink yourself into the "should have, would have, could have" stories about your debt. The real confidence builder is when you are paying it off. Sullying over the past financial decisions you made is a good way to learn from your mistakes, but never to put yourself down.

5. **Automate your financial life.** This key strategy is simple and requires unconscious effort. Saving, investing, and eliminating debt can all be done with minimum time. Consider having a certain amount of money automatically deducted to

pay off your debt, save, and invest toward your retirement simultaneously. Have the majority of your money allocated toward paying off your debt. Businesses carry debt, too, but they don't forgo investing toward their future and saving money—otherwise, there's no growth.

6. **Financial professional or money buddy.** A financial professional should provide you with a comprehensive financial planning service. However, not all planners specialize in the same areas. You should interview several prospective planners before choosing the one who best meets your needs and with whom you feel comfortable. A money buddy is someone whom you trust as a friend—whom you can talk to and discuss your financial decisions and goals. Talking it out with someone you trust helps bring to light a better direction you need to take. Do you have a vision for where you want to be in three years, five years, ten years? Establishing your short- to long-term financial goals will motivate you to stay on track.

Ornella Grosz is a personal finance expert, author, speaker, and member of the NFEC Financial Literacy Curriculum Advisory Board. She's been featured as an expert for various media outlets, national television networks, and radio stations. She blogs at Moneylicious (moneylicious.org) with actionable tips for and benefits of saving, eliminating debt, entrepreneurship, splurging, and everything to do with personal finance. Follow her on Twitter at @OrnellaGrosz or on Facebook at authorOrnellaGrosz, and visit her official site at OrnellaGrosz.com.

	Secret #4 MONEY Action Grid			
Action Step	**Guidelines**	**Time to Implement**	**Simple/ Medium/ Hard**	**Fun/ Easy/ Important**
Be Grateful	Every single day write down at least one nonmonetary thing you are grateful for in your life. This will shift your thinking toward valuing important things like health, happiness, and relationships, instead of material objects.	Instant	S	FEI
Set a Budget	The only way to make progress and get your money under control is to set a budget and stick to it. Build it with a goal in mind.	1 day	M	EI
Be Honest	Don't hide debt or have a secret savings account. Get all your money out on the table and make a plan from there.	1 day	M	I
Pay with Cash	The number one rule that most every money expert I have met always emphasizes is to pay with cash. I can't argue with that.	1 day	S	EI
Avoid Retail Therapy	We often turn to shopping to ease our stress or comfort us during difficult times. This only makes our problems worse. Instead, try to replace this habit with a healthier one like exercise or journaling.	1 day	M	EI
Don't Place Blame	When you share money responsibilities, it's easy to shift negative behaviors onto your partner. But this can only make problems worse, so work together to find a solution instead of placing blame.	7 days	M	I
Look at Your Money Mindset	Review your childhood and what might be driving your money habits today. Let go of bad habits and evaluate where you can fix them.	7 days	S	I
Stop Victimizing	If you're having money problems, don't victimize yourself. Instead, take responsibility and start taking action to change your situation.	14 days	H	I
Consolidate Debt	The simpler you can make your finances, the better. Streamline your bills and get it all on paper so you can see it and plan how to manage it.	30 days	H	I
Have Goals	Every month be sure to monitor your progress and stay motivated to keep going after your goals.	30 days	M	FI
Eliminate Nonessentials	Another common tip most money experts give is to cut out anything that isn't necessary for safety, health, and everyday living. That five-dollar latte or the extra movie channel on cable can easily be nixed without making a difference in your happiness levels, but it will make a big difference over time in your bank balance, especially with the more nonessentials you can cut out.	30 days	S	EI

Remember to use GOALS when deciding which ideas to try:

Gut-Checked: It feels right.

Obtainable: You can accomplish it in a reasonable amount of time with reasonable effort.

Actionable: You can take steps to making it happen right now.

Life-Oriented: It fits with your lifestyle right now. You have the support to make it happen.

Small Steps: The goal can be broken down into multiple, tiny steps.

III.
Core Life

Secret #5
Family Matters

Creating More-Peaceful Relationships
and Less-Stressed Kids

"I think the family is the place where the most ridiculous
and least respectable things in the world go on." —Ugo Betti

Resources:

Get downloadable worksheets and
tutorials for Secret #5
Family Matters at:

HHESecrets.com

*Use your smartphone to scan the below
QR code to go there now.*

Benefits:

- Fewer arguments with spouse.
- More peaceful home environment.
- More enjoyable vacations.
- More even division of home chores.
- More free time.
- Teach kids responsibility.
- Reconnect with significant other.
- Argue more effectively.
- Let go of grudges.

What's on Tap?

Between carpools, home chores, work schedules, and kid activities, stress is inevitable. Add to that mix a child with challenges or a relationship on its last leg and you have yourself the perfect storm for anxiety and frustration. But despite these common stressors, we put on a show of perfection and happiness and sweep our stress under the rug so no one knows we are anything but pulled together and on the ball.

We all suffer with big or small stress every single day. As long as we are taking steps to keep our lives in harmony and we are heeding the warning signals our bodies give us to take a break every now and then, we are minimizing the damage stress can cause. But there are times when it all comes to a head at once. You have an unexpected car repair, a child gets in trouble at school, you get into a fight with your spouse, you have a bad day at work—and it all pushes you into a place of extreme and damaging stress. The stress chemicals circulate and don't subside, because the stress just keeps coming.

How can we take back control of stress in our relationships and for our kids so life is more peaceful and everyone in our family is healthier and happier? The Happy Hour Effect Secret #5 will reveal several ways to help your kids stress less, as well as ways you can have a better relationship with your spouse or significant other. We will learn about:

- Raising less-stressed kids
- Having a peaceful relationship
- Next steps

When times get tough at home, this chapter can help remind you how to keep your kids stress-free and your relationships happy.

Raising Less-Stressed Kids

Yep, you know it's true—we do too much and commit to too much.

And all that crazy scheduling leads to stress. In today's world, not only are our calendars bursting at the seams, but we are also committing our kids to countless activities, adding stress to their lives and our own. We can argue we want our kids to be exposed to a lot of things and be great at everything. I don't disagree. As a lifetime overachiever and over-committer, and as the mother of a five-year-old, I am right there with you. I want the very best for my child because I always sought out the best for myself. But in this quest for the best kid on the block, we are putting ourselves and our children at risk. Not only are adults experiencing more stress than ever, but kids are too. This stress is causing health problems, behavioral issues, learning challenges, and problems with social situations and relationships. We must set an example for our kids and be the role model they need to develop their own life habits as they grow into adults. Stress management is a key component of a successfully balanced and healthy life. Some of the best ways to keep kids happy, healthy, and stress-free are:

- **Limit digital entertainment.** We grew up with TV and video games. They aren't all bad. But in today's world, technology drives everything from entertainment to interpersonal communications. Texting and instant messaging have replaced phone conversations and in-person chats. Facebook has become the new hangout. And TV and video games have become the entertainment norm instead of active pastimes that keep kids engaged and off their butts. Every kid is different in what they need. It is up to you as a parent to find the happy balance where they are able to enjoy their favorite digital activities while still staying physically active for their health and well-being. If your child is overweight, shows signs of depression or antisocial behavior, or has a lack of enthusiasm for life, you must evaluate their activities and be sure they are engaging in the real world and not just a virtual world.

- **Offer a variety of activities, but not too many.** Kids are overscheduled, overworked, and overstimulated. The options for entertainment, athletics, activities, and jobs are overwhelming for parents and even more overwhelming for kids themselves. When we force our kids to participate in many activities, we are stretching them thin. We are stretching their patience. And we are stretching their attention spans. Of course we want to teach them responsibility and let them find their own course in life by experiencing a lot of different things, but it shouldn't be force-fed. Providing options without requirements is a good way to go when it comes to helping kids pick and choose how they will fill their time. Offer a diverse mix of activities that includes exercise, mental stimulation, and humanitarian aspects so they are exposed to things that will make them a well-rounded citizen of the world.

- **Let them play.** Some parents are so worried their kids will get in trouble or make bad choices that they don't give them time to just be kids. Or they are so worried their kid won't be as smart or as talented as the next kid, so they put them in everything, hoping for excellence in at least one and hopefully more. But if you are providing a solid direction with regard to morals, ethics, health, and humanity, your kids will make the right choices in life. They may make some mistakes along the way, but we need to let go and let them make them. This will make them feel much more responsible and important, rather than being forced into nonstop sports and classes. Let them be kids.

- **Redirect negative behaviors.** Instead of having an outburst when your kid does, diffuse the situation by changing the topic or path you are on. If a kid is screaming about doing a chore, change the subject to something else and readdress the chore later after the child has calmed down. If a young child is having a tantrum, let them blow off the steam. Ignore the meltdown, and once they have calmed down, talk about something else besides what set them off.

Fear and Stress

by Barb Greenberg, author and advisor

There is nothing like a dose of fear to trigger stress. Fear can paralyze you. It can keep you from making good decisions—or from making any decisions at all. It makes you believe something is wrong with you and causes you to isolate yourself. And it can find its way into every corner of your life.

My stress level shifted into high gear during my divorce because I was constantly fearful. I was afraid of being alone, of the pain I was causing my children, and of not being able to support myself. I was afraid I was eating too much and I was afraid I was not eating enough. I was afraid my mother would come over and I wouldn't have cleaned the bathroom.

Be aware that fear can disguise itself as being overcautious or indecisive. If you are waiting for all your ducks to get in a row, please know they never will. And though you can get a duck or two going, new ducks are always hatching.

Fear can also disguise itself as perfectionism, so please set the bar a little lower for yourself. Wherever you are in life, you will make the best decisions you can. They might not be perfect, but life isn't about being perfect. It's about something much more important. It's about being human.

How to ease your fears and reduce stress:

1. Understand that fear is a normal reaction to change and there is nothing wrong with you.

2. Ask for help and surround yourself with caring friends and professional support when you need it.

3. Trust in your ability, your strength, and your higher power.

4. Do the best you can, one day at a time. Your best might be to make a budget or take a nap. It might be to make that difficult phone call or have a cookie.

5. Journal about your fear. Writing can help you discover truths and insights.

6. Breathe! Take a slow, deep breath every so often during the day, especially when you start to feel overwhelmed. It's calming, it helps you stay present, and it gets some oxygen into your system all at the same time.

When you can ease your fears, you will ease your stress, and you will open up to new and brighter possibilities.

Barb Greenberg is an author, speaker, and businesswoman who offers support for women in transition, especially those dealing with divorce. Her books *Hope Grew Round Me* and *After the Ball: A Woman's Tale of Reclaiming Happily Ever After* are available exclusively at RosePathPress.com. Visit Barb's official site at BarbGreenberg.com.

- **Be aware and be there.** With all the activities in our lives, we may be lucky to have more than a few minutes of good, quality time with our kids, getting to know their personalities and interests. It may sound untrue and a little harsh, but when you think about it, kids are so busy bopping between activities, you may have greetings in the car or at mealtimes, but beyond that it's always go-go-go. Build in time to just talk and spend time doing things your child wants to do. Learn their behavioral patterns and characteristics. Really be involved and there for your child. This connection will also allow you to be aware when something is different in their lives. A slow or sudden withdrawal could mean problems at school. A change in eating habits could mean a health problem. Stay engaged and observant.

- **Be a great role model.** The best way you can keep your kids happy, healthy, and stress-free is to live that way yourself. They will mirror your behaviors, so be sure you are living how you envision your children living their lives. Eat healthfully. Exercise. Have fun. Leave work at the office. Play hard. Live your own life. Teach them responsible and respectful behaviors. Imagine how you want them to live when they are adults, and then live that way yourself.

All kids are different and require their own special guidance and parenting tactics. Don't be afraid to experiment and try different approaches and techniques until you find the right combination that brings out the best in your child and the best in you.

Having a Peaceful Relationship

The divorce rate is sky high. Arguments abound. The sparks die out. There is no doubt about it that relationships are hard and stressful. Before my husband died, we were nine months into first-time parenthood. And for those of you who have had kids, you know how challenging that first year after the first child is born can be. I had heard the stories of couples whose relationships unraveled as soon as the baby arrived and dominated their time and energy. Money problems arise and we run. Temptation leads us astray and we make bad decisions.

In short, we allow outside influences to control the happiness and potential outcome of our relationships. We forget about those things that attracted us to the person in the first place and let other responsibilities and tasks take priority over the person who we are supposed to rely on for physical, mental, and emotional well-being. Over the years I have heard so many stories of couples whose relationships went south for ridiculous reasons. I've also heard very serious stories of relationships that eroded for very real and valid reasons. Regardless of why relationships suffer or fail, there are ways to find a path back to each other, despite the stress and pressure that we face every day.

- **Communicate.** This is the first thing that therapists and relationship experts say when asked how couples can improve their relationships. But communicating is easier said than done, especially when men and women are so different in so many ways. And yet, that is the first step to a happier relationship. You must let go of your pride and stubbornness and be honest with your partner. If you don't, guilt, anger, and frustration will build up and eventually blow. At the first sign of discontent or stress, lay it all out on the table.

- **Plan how to argue.** This may sound strange, but early in your relationship (or now) make a plan for how you will handle conflicts together. Before stress or disagreement sets in, have a discussion about how you will work through issues and what approach you will take to solve them.

- Agree together that you will allow the other to **speak openly and freely without judgment**. Expect the same from them.

- Agree that you may disagree but that you will try to **find common ground.**

- Agree that neither of you will claim to be right, because **there are two sides** to every situation.

- When stress or an argument begins, **move to a conducive locale** where you can discuss things calmly and openly. This might mean going to a public place if one or both of you tend to fly off the handle. If you're in public, it may mean going home if you need the privacy to discuss a sensitive issue.

- **Remember the love.** So many times when stress sets in, we dwell on the negative. Our minds naturally create worst-case scenarios, and our partners get lumped into it. When going through tough times, go back to the beginning of your relationship and try to recreate that relationship again. Remember what attracted you to the person. Remind yourself of their best attributes.

Life is hard—and so is love. Finding that perfect person who was made just for you is a discovery process. And the journey will change throughout your lifetime. Be kind and respectful to yourself and kind and respectful to your partner. You both deserve it no matter how bad an argument or how dire a circumstance may seem.

Now What?

Families and relationships are complicated. Sometimes those we love the most are the same people we treat the worst, especially when hard times roll around, as they inevitably do at some point in everyone's lives. But with some easy shifts to how we interact with our kids and significant others, we can live lives of harmony and happiness. Use one or all of the ideas in this chapter to help you get there.

"Children know when their parents are stressed out, and they feel sad about it. Kids want happy, stress-free parents. While it may not be possible to create a completely stress-free life, healthy stress management can be modeled to our children. Parents can easily incorporate deep breathing and positive stress-reducing statements into their lives and family routines. Parents and children who use stress management will experience less stress and more joy!"

—Lori Lite, founder of Stress Free Kids

Lori Lite is the founder of Stress Free Kids and has created a line of books and CDs designed to help children, teens, and adults decrease stress, anxiety, and anger. Ms. Lite's books, CDs, and lesson plans are considered a resource for parents, psychologists, therapists, child life specialists, teachers, and yoga instructors. Lori is a certified children's meditation facilitator and Sears' Manage My Life parenting expert. Learn more at: StressFreeKids.com

Secret #5 FAMILY Action Grid

Action Step	Guidelines	Time to Implement	Simple/ Medium/ Hard	Fun/ Easy/ Important
Remember the Love	Every relationship has challenges, but they all started somewhere great (well, hopefully they did). When bad times hit, recreate your early relationship, think about those characteristics that you love in the other person, and forget about the flaws that drive you crazy sometimes.	Instant	S	FEI
Be Aware and Be There	Get engaged in your child's life by sitting down on the floor to play or going out and doing things together that *they* choose. Really get to know their personality and health so when things go astray, you will be aware of it. Be an integral part of their lives, not just an observer, chauffeur, and chef.	Instant	S	FEI
Be a Role Model	The best way to teach kids and others to stress less and be healthier and happier is to live that way yourself.	Instant	S	FEI
Communicate	Be a great listener. Don't always lecture or nag. Let your kids and spouse talk openly without judgment.	1 day	M	I
Offer Kids Variety but Not Too Much	Provide different options for activities, but don't overload them with so much stuff they feel overwhelmed. Don't over-schedule.	1 day	S	FEI
Let Kids Play	Give kids time to just be kids. Let them run around and have unstructured play time. Don't schedule their lives down to the very minute. It will stress them and you.	1 day	S	FEI
Limit Digital Entertainment	Keep your kids active with outdoor play, games, and reading, instead of video games, TV, mobile apps, and the Internet. They will get more physical activity and learn to relate to people one-on-one as opposed to digitally.	7 days	S	EI
Plan How to Argue	Early in any relationship, have a plan for how you will argue. Agree in advance that you will both be open to hearing the other's opinions. Agree that small issues won't blow up into giant blowouts.	7 days	M	EI
Redirect Negative Behavior	When a tantrum or sass sets in, ignore it or redirect it by changing the path you are on. Don't get into a battle or argument. If you aren't making progress, just walk away until you are both calm again.	14 days	H	I
Find Common Ground	There are three sides to every story: your side, the other person's side, and the right story. Be sure you aren't forcing your agenda, and try to find agreement on at least one point of any argument.	14 days	H	I
Don't Judge	When arguments arise, don't judge the other person. Agree in advance that you are both going to be given the chance to speak your mind, and then you will calmly and rationally discuss next steps.	30 days	M	I

Remember to use GOALS when deciding which ideas to try:
Gut-Checked: It feels right.
Obtainable: You can accomplish it in a reasonable amount of time with reasonable effort.
Actionable: You can take steps to making it happen right now.
Life-Oriented: It fits with your lifestyle right now. You have the support to make it happen.
Small Steps: The goal can be broken down into multiple, tiny steps.

Secret #6
Operation Body

Why Nurturing Our Physical Selves Reduces Stress

"A smiling face is half the meal." —Latvian proverb

Resources:

Get downloadable worksheets and tutorials for Secret #6 Operation Body at:

HHESecrets.com

Use your smartphone to scan the below QR code to go there now.

Benefits:

- You will look better.
- Your body will be stronger.
- You will have more energy.
- You will sleep better.
- Happiness levels will increase.
- Stress will decrease.
- More self-confidence.
- Others will perceive you in a more positive way.
- Teach kids good habits.
- Appear more attractive to the opposite sex.
- Have fewer health problems.
- Make your doctor very, very happy.

What's on Tap?

Yoga, Atkins, Paleo, spinning, Weight Watchers, celeb trainers—the list of diet plans, exercise programs, and tools that we can tap into to lose weight, look better, and be healthier goes on and on. You've probably tried a lot of them over the years. The problem is that most are not sustainable over the long term, and once we try one and fail, our stress levels skyrocket because we feel guilty and unsuccessful. We go back to our old habits and the weight returns.

Stress is the culprit of many of our body woes. It affects our skin, hair, nails, weight, and overall appearance in more ways than I can count. But if we can manage to get our stress under control, we can also get our weight and body issues under control. The secret is to spend a little time every day on nurturing our physical bodies through exercise, diet, and laughter with the goal of looking better, feeling better, and experiencing less stress in the process.

There are thousands of diets, exercise plans, and tools to live a healthier lifestyle. But how do we decide which will work best to not only be healthy but to stress less in the process? The Happy Hour Effect Secret #6 will give you the insight you need to make the best choices for your physical body. We will learn about:

- Happy mood foods
- Laughter
- Exercise
- Next steps

We must make choices every day about our wellness. This chapter will help us to nurture our bodies and relieve stress in the process.

How Can I Physically Stress Less?

There are several ways to physically counteract stress that can be accomplished through diet, exercise, laughter, or a combination of tactics.

1. **Eliminate Stress.** This strategy works by actually removing the stress-causing situation from your life. It may be quitting a committee that stresses you out or removing a trivial item from your to-do list. This tactic works because you are never initiating the stress response in the first place, so stress chemicals aren't released to cause damage.

2. **Reduce Stress.** This works by lowering the amounts of stress chemicals in your body or limiting the damage that they cause by reducing symptoms of stress. This may include things like working stress chemicals out of your body faster through exercise, or lowering your blood pressure and relaxing muscles by meditating or laughing.

3. **Counteract Stress.** This strategy helps to balance out the stress response by either repairing or preventing the damage from stress, or participating in activities that stimulate the release of endorphins and other feel-good chemicals in your body. The stress chemicals may not go away, but they will be diluted or slowed by the happiness-inducing effects of your activities. This could mean eating antioxidant-rich foods that help repair or prevent cell damage from the stress chemicals. Or it could be getting a good belly laugh from a hilarious movie to boost the feel-good chemicals in your body.

Happy Mood Foods

There are so many ways to eat more healthfully *and* help reduce stress at the same time. And once your body is functioning on healthy fuel from natural and unprocessed foods, the stress response will naturally subside. But it's difficult to wade through the information out there in the media and from food companies to decide what is really healthy.

Eat and Move for Less Stress

by Jina Schaefer, diet and exercise expert

When dealing with stress and how if affects your body, you need to look deeper. Your body has not evolved much from your prehistoric ancestors. Your body is evolving at a much slower pace than today's food, technology, and stresses. Because of this, it will take a little extra effort and planning to better deal with stress and stay healthy. More work, but the benefits are well worth it!

When you are stressed, your body releases stress hormones adrenaline and cortisol. Adrenaline and cortisol increase heart rate and blood pressure, constrict blood vessels, and dilate air passages, among other things. This response works well if your stress is about gathering enough food for your loved ones, getting through a snowstorm, or outrunning the saber-toothed tiger. In other words, this response to stress is appropriate if your stress is short-term. Today, stress is long-term. Stress today is about deadlines and projects at work, hectic schedules with family and friends, health, finances, and so on. Having even low levels of stress hormones in your body continuously causes damage to your cells. This damage can manifest in many different ways, including suppressed immunity, slowed healing time, weight gain, increased appetite and cravings, higher blood pressure and heart rate, restless sleep, mood swings, a poor attitude and outlook... and more stress!

In order to prevent this damage or bounce back from it, you need to flush out the stress hormones. This will help better your mood, reduce cravings, and strengthen your cells. One of the best ways to do this is to increase your physical activity and eat for nutrition. By physical activity, I mean *any* physical activity: long or short, difficult or easy. Whether this is an hour in the gym or a five-minute walk, physical activity releases endorphins, a process which flushes stress hormones out of your body and improves your mood, lowers your cravings, and burns calories to help control your weight.

Eating for stress relief includes eating more nutrition via natural, less-processed foods such as fruits, vegetables, nuts, seeds, whole grains, and small amounts of lean cuts of meat (if any meat at all). Aim for foods with fewer ingredients. This means they have more nutrients and are closer to the plant or animal they once were. More nutrition strengthens cells so they can become more resilient to the toll stress has on your body and mind.

When it comes to adding in more nutrition and physical activity into your life, make small changes over time. Add in short walks throughout the day, take the stairs when you can, or add in a stretch break every couple of hours. For nutrition, slowly add in more fruits and vegetables to your snacks and meals. Exchange processed meats with lean cuts of meat or nuts or seeds. Exchange processed carbohydrates for whole grain options.

Jina Schaefer is the founder of Discover Health. Since 2002 she has helped hundreds of people reach and maintain their weight loss and wellness goals. She believes in getting people happier and healthier with realistic and sustainable methods. Explore more at MyDiscoverHealth.com.

The easiest way to decide if you should eat something is to determine how natural the food is and where it came from. You want to eat things that are as close to their original source as possible. For example, an actual apple is much better than applesauce or apple juice—and definitely better than apple pie. A whole rotisserie chicken is much better than chicken nuggets or lunchmeat. Unprocessed oatmeal is much better than super-processed breakfast cereal. Always look for foods with as few ingredients on the label as possible. The more natural and unprocessed a food is, the more nutrition it has packed into it. And the more nutritional substance it has, the more benefit it can have on your body.

I will spare you the biology lesson here, but foods that are rich in nutrients have a much easier time being digested, absorbed, and used by the body for energy, repair, and vitality. As foods are absorbed into our systems, our bodies need pure and powerful nutrition to fuel us effectively. If we are eating processed, chemical-laden foods, we are bathing our cells in toxicity and straining our systems that have to filter out all of the unusable junk. Some of the worst foods for our health are the most commonly purchased and consumed. Food companies create chemicals that specifically addict us to the flavors and keep us wanting and eating more. Here are some examples:

- **Breakfast cereals**: Most have mile-long ingredient lists and fake nutrients added in—plus loads of sugar and salt. Skip cereal and have oatmeal, eggs, and fruit instead.
- **Soda**: Straight chemicals with zero nutritional value. Diet sodas are bad too, so just skip them altogether. Substitute tea if you like the caffeine, or plain seltzer water or club soda with a squeeze of fruit juice if you like the fizz.
- **Chips**: Boy are these delicious, but they are uber-processed with way too much salt and artificial flavoring. Opt for nutrition-packed nuts instead for crunch and saltiness.
- **Baked goods, including white bread**: Filled with white flour and sugar, these items have no nutritional value and cause major swings in our blood sugar levels. If you need something

sweet and fluffy, try a piece of whole wheat toast with almond butter, or just have a bite from someone else.

- **Yogurt**: Unless you're buying plain, unsweetened yogurt, you are basically eating a cup full of sugar. Try plain Greek yogurt with fresh fruit and a tiny squeeze of honey or agave syrup instead.

- **Prepackaged meals**: Yes, a Lean Cuisine might be easy and seem healthy, but most are filled with salt and processed ingredients. Once a month, cook a bulk of your favorite meal and freeze it into individual portions for quick meals on the go.

- **Lunch meat**: I love me some good processed meat, but they are filled with salt, nitrates, and other preservatives. If you must have deli meats, look for low-sodium, nitrate-free, and uncured products. Better yet, skip them and use leftover chicken breast, pork, or beef for sandwiches.

- **Salad dressing**: Take a look at these ingredient lists and you will be appalled by how much goes into them. You can easily make your own dressings that are much healthier and tastier. Use balsamic, olive oil, Dijon mustard, lemon juice, herbs, and other fresh ingredients to create your own blends. My favorite is a lemon poppy seed dressing that is so tasty, I can practically drink it. Get it on the website.

It's not easy to cut out the processed foods we are so used to eating. The chemicals in them are purposely addictive and meant to keep us coming back for more. It's like kicking a smoking habit. Just stick with the good stuff. As your body gets used to less salt and chemicals, your cells will start to get healthier from the nutrient-rich foods you are eating. It will become easier and easier to make healthy choices. Here is a list of the best types of foods you should be eating to get the most nutritional benefit for your body and stress levels:

- **Fruits and vegetables**: Whether fresh or frozen, antioxidant-packed produce packs the first line of defense against cell damage.

- **Lean meats:** Our bodies need protein and iron, and lean meats are the quickest and easiest way to get it. Unless you have a restricted diet, don't be afraid to include meat in your meals—just limit it to once or twice a day.
- **Fish:** These powerhouses are filled with omegas and other nutrients that can help lower the risk of heart disease and protect us from stress. Load up on these several times per week.
- **Beans:** A great substitute for meat and a great addition to any diet, beans are filled with fiber and protein to help keep our systems running smoothly.
- **Nuts:** These are a crunchy and delicious substitute for salty snacks. Plus they have antioxidants, fiber, and trace nutrients.
- **Red wine:** You didn't think I would deny you a cocktail, did you? Red wine is filled with good stuff like resveratrol, a powerful antioxidant found in the skins of grapes. So go ahead and indulge—just stick to a glass or two.
- **Dark chocolate:** More good stuff! Dark chocolate has antioxidants that help protect our cells from damage. Savor a square every day!

Laughter

Do you remember the last time you laughed so hard you could hardly breathe? I do. My daughter was getting dressed in her snow gear to go outside to play. We had just purchased new snowpants to go with a big, puffy, purple jacket that was filled with down for extra warmth. She put the pants and jacket on and both were a little too big. She looked down at her hands and said, "My hands look so tiny," as she wiggled her little fingers. She did look like the marshmallow man, and we both busted out laughing, continuing for about fifteen minutes with tears of laughter and all. In hindsight, it's not that funny, but at the time, we found humor in an everyday situation. The rest of the day was happy and fun because the feel-good endorphins that were released by our brains during that laughing session stuck with us and

Chocolate for Less Stress

by Max and Ally Sinclair, chocolatiers at
Cocopotamus by NYDC Chocolate

Life always has its ups and downs. It must. That's what makes life interesting. And when it gets a little too "interesting," chocolate helps! Here's how:

Chocolate is satisfying; it is "good food." (We know we want it!) Chocolate tastes best when we let it slowly melt in our mouths, tasting its smoothness, its depth of flavor, its subtle nuances—sweet, bitter, spicy, nutty, fruity. As we grow older, we realize that happiness is treasuring small moments of joy. Bit by bit. Like savoring chocolate. It is these little moments of joy throughout our hectic day that help us releases stress.

We love the flavor of chocolate, don't we? It is rich, complex, heady stuff, and most of us crave it. Here's a little known fact: much like wine and coffee, chocolate contains an astonishingly high number of what is called "flavor components." There are fifteen hundred of them, to be precise. This amazing depth of flavor is made even more delicious by the fact that the melting point of chocolate is the same as the temperature of the human body. Chocolate melts in your mouth so easily for that reason, releasing its heady mixture of yumminess. No wonder biting into deep, rich chocolate is a lot like falling in love again.

Chocolate is good for the mood! As many of you might already know, chocolate naturally releases endorphins in your body. Dark chocolate, especially, has also been shown to help lower high blood pressure while providing a good dose of healthy antioxidants. The result? A happier, healthier you.

Chocolate connects us; that's good for the soul. It connects us to our past, with those fun childhood memories, like Grandma's classic chocolate chip cookies or licking the beaters after mixing up some chocolate brownies with your sis. Chocolate also connects us to others, as we love to give and receive chocolate gifts. And it connects us to traditions and holidays. Our connection to others and our loved ones enriches our lives and extends our gratitude.

At our company, Cocopotamus, we use chocolate to spread our own agenda. Namely: joy. Joy, to the world. We put a modern twist on the great American tradition of fudge, handcrafting dark chocolate fudge truffles infused with amazing flavors from around the country and around the world. So, for us, "joy to the world" is our true mission—chocolate is the perfect vehicle to deliver it. And it is perfectly delicious!

Max and Ally Sinclair are the founders of Cocopotamus by NYDC Chocolate. Their amazing truffles are sold across the country and have been featured at celebrity events in Hollywood and in media across the country. Learn more and order chocolate at cocopotamus.com.

kept circulating even though the actual situation was over.

The same thing can happen after any feel-good situation. A good belly laugh. A dance party. Singing at the top of your lungs. A funny movie. Anything that gets you smiling will get you less stressed. Here are some ideas you can do by yourself, with your kids, or with anyone else you can round up for a good laugh:

- Laughter yoga (Yes, this is a real thing!)
- Funny movies
- Karaoke or singing
- Dancing
- Breakdancing (Seriously—try it! I dare you to keep a straight face.)
- Joke-off with kids
- Read the comics in the newspaper
- Go for happy hour with a funny friend
- Staring contest (This one guarantees laughs *every* time.)
- Make silly faces
- Video games requiring active participation (movement, trivia, etc.)
- Board games (I love Scattergories, Apples to Apples, and Balderdash.)
- Play dress-up (even adults can do this)

Making time for laughter and fun is so important to balance out the tough stuff that we face in life. For more ideas to get you smiling and get the feel-good chemicals flowing, check out Secret #12.

Exercise

I dislike exercise. It is just so much work, and I would rather spend my time eating, writing, reading, or doing something fun—anything other than sweating. And yet, I know it's important for my health, so I force myself to do it. Whenever I do, I feel fantastic afterwards. This post-workout buzz is caused by the release of endorphins that make us feel good physically and mentally. These feel-good chemicals also help to counteract stress chemicals that are circulating, *and* exercise helps to circulate those stress chemicals out of you faster.

Exercising is clearly good for attacking stress head on, but it can also work wonders in not so obvious ways. Exercise is great for our skin. The sweating and heat increases blood circulation and gives us a rosy, healthy glow. Exercise also sculpts our bodies into healthy shapes that boost our confidence levels. And you know the old saying: when you look good, you feel good, and when you feel good, you look good! There really is no substitute for super effective stress relief and super effectiveness in boosting confidence than good ol' exercise.

The good news for fellow exercise despisers like me is that it doesn't take hours and hours of time or buckets of sweat to make a difference. Even just a few minutes a couple of times a day can help keep your weight stable, reduce stress, and improve your confidence. Here are some super simple ways to sneak more exercise into your day:

- Take the steps.
- Do sit-ups or push-ups during TV commercial breaks.
- Park at the back of parking lots.
- Walk around the block after lunch.
- Lift weights while you watch your favorite TV show.
- Do calf raises (go up and down on your tippy toes) while cooking dinner.
- Sit on an exercise ball instead of a chair at your desk. (Trust me—this one is a game changer.)
- Do stretches at your desk a couple of times a day.
- Have a dance party with your kids.
- Play video games that require movement (sports, dance games, fitness games).
- Pace around the house when talking on the phone.

If you can learn to move more and lie around less, you will be well on your way to a healthier body and lower stress levels.

Now What?

Keeping your body healthy is the easiest way to fight the damaging effects of stress. Strong muscles, nutrient-dense foods, and a brain releasing endorphins, all rolled into one body, is the perfect stress fighter. But don't take it from me. Experience it yourself by trying some of these ideas for a healthier body and a happier life.

Stress Less Tip

"I started running a couple of years ago, and I find that it is one of the few times that I am alone, enjoying the outdoors, appreciating my body, and able to really hear myself breathe. For that thirty or forty minutes, everything else disappears."
—Kim Pirrella, host of NotSoSoccerMom™ Radio Network, NotSoSoccerMomRadio.com, @kimpirrella on Twitter

Secret #6 OPERATION BODY Action Grid

Action Step	Guidelines	Time to Implement	Simple/ Medium/ Hard	Fun/ Easy/ Important
Laugh	The best and most powerful stressbuster is a good laugh. You stimulate muscles to boost energy. You release endorphins (feel-good chemicals), which counteract stress. And when you smile, people just react more positively to you.	Instant	S	FEI
Move More	You don't have to train for a marathon or lift major weights to get health benefits. Just move more by taking the steps, going for a walk over lunch, parking as far from the mall entrance as possible, etc. Over time, your body will want more exercise and you will be prepared to move.	Instant	S	FEI
Skip Junk	Junk food tastes good and makes you feel good—temporarily. But a sugar crash and the chemicals in junk food can wreak havoc on your body. So indulge occasionally, but opt for healthy most of the time.	1 day	M	EI
Load Up on Antioxidants	Eat foods rich in antioxidants that can help protect your body from the damage caused by stress. Things like fresh fruits, vegetables, nuts, and seeds are loaded with them, so add multiple servings to every meal or have for snacks.	1 day	S	FEI
Eat Fish	Omega 3s have been found to help ease the symptoms of depression—plus they help protect your heart and cardiovascular system, which are extremely strained during stress.	1 day	S	EI
Have Small Goals	Set up small, easy goals to keep you motivated to make positive changes to your health habits.	1 day	S	FEI
Indulge	Eating a healthy diet is important for stress management and health, but be sure to build in cheat meals and treats every now and then. Deprivation is never a good thing.	7 days	S	FEI

Remember to use GOALS when deciding which ideas to try:

Gut-Checked: It feels right.

Obtainable: You can accomplish it in a reasonable amount of time with reasonable effort.

Actionable: You can take steps to making it happen right now.

Life-Oriented: It fits with your lifestyle right now. You have the support to make it happen.

Small Steps: The goal can be broken down into multiple, tiny steps.

Secret #7
To the Mattresses

Sleep and Sex for Less Stress (Oh yah—we are going there!)

"One of the most adventurous things left is to go to bed, for no one can lay a hand on our dreams." —E.V. Lucas

"Sex ought to be a wholly satisfying link between two affectionate people from which they emerge unanxious, rewarded, and ready for more." —Alex Comfort

Resources:

Get downloadable worksheets and tutorials for Secret #7 Me-Time at:

HHESecrets.com

Use your smartphone to scan the below QR code to go there now.

Benefits:

- More energy throughout the day.
- Increased blood flow.
- Happier attitude.
- More connected to significant other.
- Less likely to get sick.
- Less irritability at work and at home.
- Fall asleep faster.
- Sleep more deeply.

What's on Tap?

Did you know that quality time between the sheets, whether sleeping or partaking in a little horizontal mambo, can reduce stress? Yep—a little extra sleep and a little (or a lot) more sex can work wonders in the de-stressing department.

But today, lots of things get in the way of solid sleep, like looming to-do lists and the runaway mind that can keep us awake. And our desire for sex can be just as affected by time crunches, headaches, kids, or just not being in the mood. And while sleep and sex are both powerful stress-less tools, we aren't making them a priority.

The Happy Hour Effect Secret #7 will uncover the reasons sleep is so important and why sex helps us to stress less too. We will learn:

- Why sleep?
- The get-some-sleep mindset
- Why sex?
- Bedroom prep 101
- Next steps

With just a few shifts in your bedroom habits, you will discover that less stress isn't the only benefit from getting more sleep and more sex.

Why Sleep?

One of the most overlooked areas of our life is sleep. It is during those precious hours of slumber that we heal, rejuvenate, and relax physically, mentally, and emotionally. Imagine the last time you had a big argument with your significant other or you had a bad day at work. You likely went to bed stewing and fretting over it, but then, miraculously, the next morning you hardly remembered what you were annoyed at in the first place. Or when you are fighting a cold, how healing it is to just spend a day or two in bed. Our bodies need sleep to function well, and our brains need sleep to keep us happy and energized.

Even losing a little sleep can impact you the next day. And lost sleep over time leads to a major sleep deficit that can lead to serious health concerns, suffering productivity, and strained relationships. Sleep is necessary to allow the body the time it needs to find its happy place again. During the day we are bombarded by stressors, environmental toxins, difficult people, to-do lists, and all of the other responsibilities that pull on us. This constant demand on us depletes our energy and increases stress chemicals in the body. At night when we sleep, we are allowing our bodies to rest and calm down. We are able to temporarily forget about our anxiety and schedule and instead, just sleep. The stress chemicals subside. Our worries subside. The stress subsides. But when we shortchange ourselves and don't get the sleep we need, we aren't able to get fully back to the place of balance that our bodies need in order to operate at their maximum potential.

Instead, we are a sleep-deprived nation living on caffeine and fast food to get us through the day. When we finally get home, we stay up too late, lie awake with monkey mind trying to fall asleep, toss and turn once we do fall asleep, and then wake up just a few short hours later to do it all over again. We never give ourselves the time we need and deserve to just sleep. Whether it's kids, schedules, home chores, or a TV or Internet addiction, we are lured from our beds by nagging responsibilities. We are unable or unwilling to let today's to-do list carry over until tomorrow so we can hit the hay at a decent hour. But with just a few small changes to your attitude, to-do list, and bedtime routine, you will be well on your way to a great night's sleep in no time.

The Get-Some-Sleep Mindset

When I ask people I work with what they wish they could change about their life, one of the most common answers is they wish they had more hours in the day. Unfortunately, this will never happen. We need to learn to work with the hours we have and give our bodies the time needed to reenergize and heal. The first step is to get a handle

Stress: You Have a Choice

by Lynette Crane, MA, CTACC

Over the past few decades, information on stress management has mushroomed into a huge field. Yet, with all this attention, stress hasn't gone away. In fact, it is now estimated that 85 percent of sickness is due to stress.

Luckily, we now know that only 10 percent of stress is due to what happens to us; 90 percent is due to how we *think* about what happens to us. The good news is that we can change that.

First, make sure that when you are faced with stress—a job change, a deadline, moving, etc.—you get enough deep, restful sleep. Make it your top priority. Sleep deprivation sets you up for stress, increases your craving for sugar, fat, and salt, and decreases your motivation to exercise. Good sleep can make molehills out of mountains.

Second, you must remember that "stress makes you stupid," which means that, under stress, you make stupid choices. Here's a way to slow down and consider more options, using the **StressBuster Formula** I teach all my clients: pause, breathe, choose.

Pause: That's all. When you feel irritated, angry, sad, or just plain rushed, just say "stop it" to yourself.

Breathe: Let the muscles of your chest and belly go and breathe in slowly to the count of four, letting your entire body fill with air like a slowly inflating balloon. Then exhale for four counts. Repeat several times.

Choose: Look at how you are responding to the situation, then ask yourself a question or two, such as: "In the long run, what really counts?" or "How bad will it be if I am a few minutes late?"

Practice this little formula daily in minor stressful situations, such as being stuck in traffic, because the more you practice it, the more expert you will become at handling the big stressors when they come along.

Lynette Crane is a speaker, writer, and coach. She is an expert on stress solutions, peak performance, shyness, and self-esteem. She is the founder of Creative Life Changes and creator of "30 Steps to Serenity" and "A Journey to Your Islands of Peace." Find detailed tips on getting deep, restful sleep, as well as creative ways to think your way to serenity, at: CreativeLifeChanges.com on your to-do list so you're not going over and over it in your mind when trying to sleep. Take a read of the Prioritization secret for some ideas to get your daily tasks under control. Next, prepare yourself for sleep by welcoming it into your day. Many of us fight against going to bed until the very moment we have to shut the light off and shut our eyes. Finally, take steps to allow your body to fully rest. Having a pre-bedtime routine can help you mentally and physically prepare for quality and quantity time asleep. Here are some ways to get more and better sleep (use these tips for kids too!):

- Check your to-do list for the day and move unfinished tasks to tomorrow.
- Avoid caffeine any time after lunch.
- Exercise early in the day.
- Do some light stretching an hour or two before bedtime.
- Shut off electronics at least an hour before bedtime.
- Do some deep breathing or meditation before bed—even if just for a minute or two.
- Try aromatherapy.
- Have a cup of herbal tea, like chamomile.
- Get nice sheets so it's a treat to turn in.
- Wear nice pajamas so it's fun to get ready for bed.
- Go to bed an hour earlier.
- Set out your clothes and anything else you need for the next day.
- Have a routine. Do things in the same order every night so your body and mind are cued that bedtime is impending.
- Block out all light from the bedroom.
- Turn down the thermostat. Cooler temperatures signal the body for sleep.
- Use a sound machine.
- Don't allow pets onto the bed.
- Set an alarm so you're not tempted to wake to look at the clock.

As a lifetime insomniac, I can't tell you how many different experiments I have tried to make sleep come easier and last longer. Over time, I have discovered the tricks I need to use from the list above to ensure a good night's rest. For you, it will require your own experimentation to find the right combo of tools to help you sleep better. And once you find that magic combination, your energy levels will increase, your health will improve, and your stress levels will decrease.

Sex for Less Stress

Most of us can't imagine uttering the word sex out loud to ourselves, let alone having a discussion about its life-transforming powers with others. But it is true that a good (or even not-so-good) roll in the hay can get the feel-good juices and energy flowing. Unfortunately, sex often falls to the bottom of the priority list, especially during times of stress and busyness—the times we need to "get busy" the most! In fact, during sex, one of the most primal parts of our brains is activated—the limbic system. It is responsible for emotions, drives, love, and lust. During and after orgasm, our brains release lots and lots of endorphins (pleasure chemicals) and oxytocin (also known as the cuddle hormone). Endorphins relax you and oxytocin makes you feel more connected to your partner. In fact, the more you have sex, the more bonded you feel because of the oxytocin, which helps to strengthen and deepen your relationship. So by partaking in the act of lovemaking (or lust-making), you are naturally boosting your happiness and relaxation. Plus, the physical activity of getting the heart pumping helps to circulate stress chemicals like cortisol and adrenaline out of the body faster.

It's like exercise. Getting motivated to work out is the hardest part, but once you have your workout gear on, it's much easier to get started. Once you get going, it's much easier to keep going, and after you're done, you're so happy you just did it. Sex is the same way. At the end of a long day, the last thing many of us want is to put forth any type of effort. A couch, baggy pajamas, and a glass of wine is pure pleasure at that moment in time. But once you get mentally prepared for sex and prepped for some action, it's much easier to actually take action. And once you get started, it ends up being fun and relaxing too. And just like exercise, when it's over, you're usually so glad you did it. How can you get over the hump (pun intended) to get to a place where sex is something you look forward to instead of something you try to avoid? And what steps can you take to get in the mood in the first place?

Sex Is Fun—Just Do It

When it comes to sex, there are endless excuses we use to get out of it. Both men and women are guilty of it, and it afflicts both married and single people, young and old, gay or straight. Yes, it's true that if you ask a college guy to do it, he'll probably have his pants dropped in the blink of an eye. But when it comes to experiencing the joys of the bedroom blitz and bedroom bliss, more often than not, it's not a high priority when life gets busy.

Making the shift from a not-tonight-dear mentality to let's-get-it-on mode is easier said than done. But with practice comes the desire for more practice. We aren't striving for perfection here. It's supposed to be fun and mood-boosting, not a lot of dreaded work. That doesn't mean you can just sit (or lie) back and just enjoy the ride. Sometimes it does, but it's a two-way street. The more both parties can be engaged, the better and more fun it will be. Here are some ideas to shift your thinking and make sex a priority:

- **Do it at a different time of day.** If you're too tired at night, that will put the brakes on any progress you or your partner want to make in the bedroom department. Try it when you first wake up, and don't forget the fun of an afternoon delight.
- **Try a little roleplay.** It could be any situation you desire. Or act out that fantasy you read in a book. Be creative.
- **Try a new location.** Get out of the bedroom and try the shower, couch, or even the car or a private backyard. The thrill of a different locale can rev up your engine.

Sexy Stress Relief

by Tina B. Tessina, psychotherapist and author

Sex will not only keep your love energized; it's also fun exercise, a great stress releaser, and aerobic—it raises your heart rate and your respiration, and you don't even notice you're working hard. As you probably know, exercise reduces stress; it's an opportunity to physically express pent-up emotion. Sex also usually involves orgasm, which is a phenomenal stress releaser. Orgasm involves stressing muscles and then suddenly releasing them, to the point where the entire body is completely relaxed, which can eliminate a lot of pent-up stress. Sex involves deep breathing, which is also proven to reduce stress. Affection and touch are also relaxing and stress-reducing because they flood the system with oxytocin and other hormones associated with feelings of well-being and relaxation.

Tina B. Tessina, PhD, (a.k.a. Dr. Romance) is a thirty-plus-year psychotherapist and author of thirteen books, including *Money, Sex, and Kids: Stop Fighting about the Three Things That Can Ruin Your Marriage* and *Love Styles: How to Celebrate Your Differences*. Visit her official site at: TinaTessina.com

- **Set goals.** It may sound silly, but if you can make a game out of it, you can spice it up. See who can orgasm first or who can hold off the longest. Or try to do it every single day for a week and see what happens.
- **Try new positions.** Check out websites for ideas or just get creative.
- **Don't be embarrassed about your body.** If you have both decided together to have sex, neither of you cares about a little cellulite or too much hair somewhere.
- **Meditate with your partner.** Getting to a deeper level of relaxation with or without your partner will get you in the mood faster.

Don't be afraid to communicate openly with your partner and just relax. Sex should be fun and not something that stresses you out. Remember the benefits it has and that can help you make the shift from ho-hum to more-please in no time.

Setting the Mood

A little candlelight, some massage oil, and rose petals should do it, right? Wrong! Those things are all well and good, but they can be a little cheesy and overdone if not executed properly. Instead, think of mood setting more as creating a comfortable, relaxing space where you can let go of your inhibitions and worries. So many people are self-conscious about their bodies, and they let that hamper their sexual interactions. And I can't count how many times I've heard the excuse that the kids are to blame. It's time to cut out the excuses and develop habits that get you in the mood. Here are some ideas:

- **Wear attractive undergarments every day, not just for sex.** There are so many options for sexy *and* comfortable underwear these days that there is no excuse for granny panties or big, white old man briefs. If you have that little sexiness layer under your clothes, you will have that little extra boost of confidence.

- **Break out the champagne (or other sexy beverage).** Sharing a cocktail or mocktail with your bedmate can add a level of connection and help relax you before heading under the sheets.
- **Be clean.** This may sound a little silly or maybe a little gross, but keep yourself well groomed and hygienic. If you haven't showered for a couple of days, you're probably a little pungent and will be self-conscious about your odors. Or your partner will be less inclined to want to get intimate with you.
- **Schedule sex.** This may sound like the most unsexy mood killer there is, but actually, having a space and time set aside just for the act will get you thinking about it in advance and set your brain and body up for the impending date. The anticipation will get you revved up.
- **Take vacations.** Or at least send the kids to grandma's house for a night every once in a while. Having a longer period of uninterrupted time to connect and relax can up the sex potential and satisfaction.
- **Don't worry about the kids.** They will be exposed to sex in their lives. You can't hide it. Knowing their parents love one another is a very positive way to show them that a healthy relationship includes sex. Obviously don't flaunt it, but doing it in the privacy of your own bedroom or bathroom when the kids are occupied or asleep is perfectly acceptable.
- **Be a little naughty.** Just because you're a good girl or boy who goes to church and has some kids doesn't mean you can't exercise a little naughtiness every once in a while. It doesn't make you a bad person—just a normal one with desires and drives. Be open to healthy and safe experimentation and just have fun.
- **Have clean sheets.** This may seem strange since you'll just be dirtying them up again, but the allure of crisp, clean sheets can be very powerful.

- **Create a sexy environment.** This will differ for everyone, but experiment with lighting, music, scent, and taste. Use candles. Try flavored oils. Create a get-busy playlist on your iPod. Don't be afraid to mix it up.

Try a few of these tips to get yourself in the mood for sex and intimacy. If you aren't with a partner right now, you can still partake in self-pleasuring. It's nothing to be ashamed of and is a great substitute when the real thing isn't a possibility right now. Plus it gives you the chance to get to know yourself and what makes you feel the sexiest and turned on. You can teach those things to your next partner for an even better experience.

Sex is super powerful for stress relief and shouldn't be ignored just because it is a taboo topic to talk about in public. Hey, I'm not saying you should shout from the rooftops that you're sexing it up to relieve stress, but shouting with a partner may not be such a bad idea.

Now What?

Spending time with someone you love (or like enough to disrobe for) can be an amazing stress reliever, just like a great night's sleep can spin a stressful situation into a peaceful one. If you can learn to enjoy your bedroom time for both sleep and sex, you are one step closer to less stress. Here's a recap of things you can try to get yourself in the mood for the big O or some zzzs:

Secret #7 SLEEP AND SEX Action Grid				
Action Step	**Guidelines**	**Time to Implement**	**Simple/ Medium/ Hard**	**Fun/ Easy/ Important**
Be Creative	Don't be embarrassed or afraid to make suggestions to your partner for new ideas in the bedroom. It will be a great turn-on for both of you.	1 day	M	FI
Just Do It	Even when you don't feel like having sex, just do it anyway. Once you're in the act, you will benefit from the feel-good chemicals that your body releases, and you will be much happier after you're finished.	1 day	S	FEI
Set the Mood	Use the tips from the chapter to set a romantic mood for you and your loved one. Nice sheets, a clean body and bedroom, a glass of wine—whatever helps you feel more amorous, try it.	1 day	S	FEI
Review Lists and Plan for Tomorrow	Get all of your lists and items ready for the next day. Select wardrobe for yourself and your kids. Get your work bag or children's backpacks laid out and ready to go. Scan your to-do list so you don't have to go over it while you're lying in bed.	7 days	S	I
Limit Electronics Before Bed	Shut down your phone, email, and TV at least an hour before bed to give your body and brain time to wind down.	7 days	S	EI
Use Sleep Tricks	Lower the temperature. Shut off the lights. Get into cozy pajamas. Slip into silky sheets. Have a cup of hot herbal tea. All of these little cues can prompt your body to begin relaxing.	14 days	S	FEI
Meditate Before Bed	Take five to thirty minutes to just sit and breathe deeply through your nose. You may fall asleep—or you may get your body into a more relaxed place for when it is time for bed.	21 days	S	EI
Mix Up Your Sex Life	Think outside the missionary box and try something new. New positions. New locations. Give them a try.	30 days	M	FI
Set a Bedtime Routine	Keep your pre-bed habits the same every night so your body knows that it is time for sleep.	30 days	M	EI

Remember to use GOALS when deciding which ideas to try:
Gut-Checked: It feels right.
Obtainable: You can accomplish it in a reasonable amount of time with reasonable effort.
Actionable: You can take steps to making it happen right now.
Life-Oriented: It fits with your lifestyle right now. You have the support to make it happen.
Small Steps: The goal can be broken down into multiple, tiny steps.

IV.

Passions
&
Commitments

Resources:

Get downloadable worksheets and tutorials for Secret #8 Stress and the Uglies at:

HHESecrets.com

Use your smartphone to scan the below QR code to go there now.

Benefits:

- More confident in your life and relationships.
- Perceived in a more positive way by others.
- More respect on the job.
- Better luck in the love department.
- Healthier immune system from a change in habits.
- Clearer, healthier, smoother skin.
- Vibrant, shiny hair and stronger, longer nails.
- Fewer skin breakouts and rashes.
- Weight stabilizes and extra pounds are shed.
- More energy as your body releases stress chemicals.

When you look good, you feel good, and when you feel good, you look good!

Secret #8
Stress and the Uglies

Why Stress Makes Us Fat, Less Attractive, and Age Faster,
and How to Reclaim Your Hotness

"Things are beautiful if you love them." —Jean Anouilh

What's on Tap?

The physical and emotional consequences of stress aren't always enough to prompt us to make changes to our habits and lifestyles. Sometimes it takes something more material—something that impacts our appearance—to get us motivated to make a change. When I meet with clients and speak to groups about stress, it is this exact topic that gets their attention every time. The moment I say "stress makes you fat, ugly, and age faster," the room goes still and silent as everyone leans in, terrified that their own stress is making them less attractive in some way.

The truth is, stress *does* impact our external physical appearance in so many ways. Think back to a day when you were relaxed, happy, and stress-free. If you looked in the mirror on that day, chances are you would have seen a smiling, vibrant, healthy-looking person beaming back at you. On days like that, people respond to you differently. You get more attention. Everything seems to go right. Now think back to the last time you were stressed out or upset over something happening in your life. On that day, the person staring back at you from the mirror was probably crabby-looking with dull skin, messy or unstyled hair, and definitely no smile. And on those kinds of days, it's likely that nothing seems to go right. Store clerks are jerks, work sucks, and life is just plain crummy.

Stress will do all kinds of crazy things to your appearance, and that's what this secret will reveal. Not only will I explain the five big ways stress makes us ugly, but I will also share tips on how to re-energize your appearance using stress-relief tools, beauty and health tips, and more so the wonderful you on the inside can come shining through on the outside. The Happy Hour Effect Secret #8 will change our view of stress and its impact on our appearance by revealing:

- How stress makes us sick and just plain gross
- How stress prompts skin issues
- Why stress causes wrinkles
- How stress makes us fat
- Why we don't give a hoot about our looks when we're stressed
- Simple solutions to save our appearance from stress

It's inevitable that stress will take its toll on our appearance. The ravages of time, environment, toxins, and yes, stress, will eventually catch up with us. But while we're here, we can preserve our natural beauty with just a few simple changes to our lifestyle and habits. Is the fear of aging too quickly enough to get you motivated to manage stress? I hope so. Let's learn how!

Stress And Sickness

Remember when that coworker came into the office with a hacking, phlegmy cough and continually blew his nose, sneezed, and wheezed all day long? How attractive was that? Remember the last time you had the stomach flu and caught a glimpse of your own crusty, pale reflection in the mirror on your way to heave into the toilet? Hot stuff, right? Not so much! But the fact is, when stress sets in and isn't managed properly, the immune system goes haywire and illness inevitably sets in.

Why does illness occur when we're stressed? I talked a lot earlier in this book about the biology of stress. But specifically, the same stress chemicals that cause the fight or flight reaction in us also impact our immune systems. Stressful situations prompt your body to release stress chemicals, and when that happens, our bodies automatically slow down or cease nonessential body functions to reallocate energy and resources to the body functions that are directly related to protecting us from stress. The immune system is one of the nonessential functions that get turned down when stress sets in. This decreased functioning opens you up to illness and disease.

Illness and disease are not pretty. Whether it's a short-term sickness like the cold or flu or a long-term disease like cancer or diabetes, they all zap our appearance. Bacteria, viruses, fungus, parasites, and more can take up residence when our immune system isn't strong enough to fight them off. These bugs lead to a host of symptoms that can make us not just feel but look downright nasty. Sniffly, dry, crusty noses. Hacking coughs. Pale skin. Watery, bloodshot eyes. Diarrhea. Heck, even our smell can change during illness.

Is this imagery enough to get you on the Happy Hour Effect train? How about these more severe consequences of disease? Cancer patients lose their hair with some treatments. Diabetes patients often suffer poor circulation and healing properties and end up with amputated limbs. And while we don't judge or fault the appearance of patients with these diseases, wouldn't it be great if you could take action to prevent them in the first place? Stress management is a great place to start, so take a good look in the mirror and decide that now is the time to become proactive about fighting stress!

Stress And Your Skin

Why do brides always get breakouts right before their big day? Why does the high school kid get a massive zit the day of the prom? Why do nervous nellies get the crazy red neck hives when forced into the spotlight? You got it—stress! When our bodies suffer stress, the stress chemicals can cause a very toxic environment in our bodies. The cortisol and adrenaline pump through us, doing all kinds of crazy things to our appearance. And because there are so many nerve endings in the skin, any neurological or emotional episode will impact those nerve endings, sending the skin into a frenzy.

Skin breakouts, rashes, eczema, psoriasis, hair loss, and other skin conditions can all be made worse by stress. In fact, skin disorders are tied so intimately to our emotions that there is an emerging field of medicine called psychodermatology that addresses these very issues. Our brain and skin develop from the same cells in the embryo, so there is definitely a connection between them.

So why *do* we get breakouts right before a big event? In the case of acne—one of the most widespread skin afflictions—as our bodies respond to stress leading up to a big event, one of the stress chemicals, cortisol, prompts an increase in oil production in the skin, which leads to acne breakouts. If we can learn to reduce our stress and get those stress chemicals circulated out of our bodies faster, it will improve our skin and make us healthier and happier too.

Stress and Wrinkles

The big furrow right between my eyebrows developed in the two years after my daughter was born and after my husband died. I aged ten years in just two because the stress in my life at that time changed the chemistry of my body and my skin. But why did this happen? Did my constant frown cause the wrinkle? Was there something going on in my body that made me look older? The answer is yes on both counts.

When we are under stress, we do frown more often. And it takes more muscles to frown than it does to smile. This repetition of frowning can, over time, cause wrinkles. Many of the lines on older people's faces are this type of wrinkling caused by a lifetime of facial expressions, both happy and negative.

The other factor at play in wrinkles is collagen. Collagen is a building block of skin. It gives our faces that plump, firm, and youthful appearance. Over time, collagen breaks down and our skin sags. As collagen diminishes, skin becomes less resilient and doesn't "bounce back" like it once did. When you pinch the skin on the back of a child's hand, it springs back to its original shape. When you pinch the skin on the back of an elderly person's hand, it may stay pinched for a moment before bouncing back—if it even bounces back at all. That's because the collagen is still intact and aplenty in the child but has been eroded in the older person. Another curse of the stress response is that the stress chemicals can speed up this breakdown of collagen. And you know what that means? Less collagen = more wrinkles.

As you can see, not only does the repetition of stress frowning and furrowing cause facial wrinkles, but the stress chemicals themselves actually break down the collagen that makes us appear youthful. We can age much faster than time would naturally age us if we have a stressful lifestyle. Not good! But by implementing stress management habits into your life and using some of the skin-saving secrets in this chapter, you can protect your face from the ravages of time and stress. I feel like my skin has aged backwards since I began my stress reduction work. I look younger now than I did five years ago, and I only hope I can maintain my skin as I age.

Stress Fat

When stress sets in, our bodies naturally hold on to fat. Throughout history, this is what our bodies have been known to do to preserve and protect us during times of potential danger, food shortage, cold weather, etc. When a long winter was upon them, our ancestors knew what real stress was. When sunlight hours grew shorter, the biological response was to hold on to the fat it had and hold on even tighter to the fat it took in as extra energy stores for the long, hard winter. Now that was serious stress and a smart biological response that evolution built in to protect us!

Today we stress about traffic, work, money, relationships. Rarely do we have to worry about a long, hard winter with scarce food or little heat. Yet we are in a constant state of sustained stress, which means that those stress chemicals are always circulating in us all the time. This also means that our bodies think that impending doom may be upon us, so we hold on to fat as a defense mechanism. When I worked in corporate America, I always carried a few extra pounds. When I left to focus on my own work, the pounds came right off as my stress levels came down, with no effort on my part.

If you are carrying around extra weight despite your best efforts to shed the pounds, take a look at your stress levels. If you are in a heightened state of angst and stress all the time, chances are your body is hanging on to that fat for dear life. No amount of exercise or healthy eating will get rid of it as long as you're still stressing. Take steps to relax, let go of your anxieties, and change your perspective on stress. This will signal your body to return to a normal state, and those stress chemicals will circulate out of your body. Once you can do that, the pounds are sure to decrease too.

The Stress-Induced "I Don't Give a Crap" Attitude

When I was in my early twenties, I promised myself I would never go into public without looking pulled together. Here I am, ten(ish) years later, and real life has set in along with the real stress that goes along with it. Well, I can tell you that many times I have thrown on my Ugg boots, tossed my hair back into a ponytail, and gone to the grocery store braless and makeup-less to grab a carton of milk because I was just too tired, overwhelmed, stressed, or indifferent to put the effort into making myself presentable for public viewing. I'm sure I've scared a store clerk or two in my day.

This indifference to our appearance during stressful times is evident almost everywhere you look. Disheveled moms race through the grocery store, frantically filling their carts before their kids throw a tantrum. Overwrought workers mindlessly grab fast food and chow it down like animals so they can get back to work. Out-of-love couples dine together in sweatshirts and jeans, hardly talking, with faraway looks in their eyes. All of these scenarios are true indicators of the indifference that stress can cause in our appearance. As a busy mom myself, I know the feeling of franticness, hoping to get in and out of the store without some sort of outburst from my child. As a formerly stressed worker, I was that person at McDonald's not caring what I ate or looked like because I was "just going to work, so who cares." And I've been in a relationship on the rocks where you just don't put forth the effort to look good anymore because life is just too much work, and the last thing I wanted to do was put on a cute outfit after a long day.

So how can we spin these scenarios and get back to a place where we take pride in how we look? The old saying is so true: If you look good, you feel good. And I'm not saying we should be vain or focus so much on our outward beauty. What I'm recommending is a return to the times when going out in public meant you actually put on some lipstick and looked like yourself at your best. If you feel like a lazy, fat, dowdy mom inside, chances are you will emulate that on the outside as well. But if you can dig deep and find that sexy, charming, fun, and smart woman you are underneath the mac and cheese stained shirt and unwashed hair, you *will* behave differently and *want* to look different to show the kind of person you are on the *inside*.

When stress takes hold, it's tough to gather the inner drive to take the extra time and effort to put your best face forward when you leave the house. But if you can add a little lip gloss, take off the baseball cap, comb your hair, and put on a clean shirt, you will feel better and people will relate to you in a more positive way. And that in itself will start to reduce your stress just by the fact that others are being nicer to you. Let your inner light shine instead of the oil on your T-zone. Be confident in your appearance and less stress will follow.

Boost Your Beauty for Less Stress

by Wendy Lyn Phillips, image expert and bestselling author

Not only does stress make you age more quickly and bring on the "uglies," but it's *just plain ugly*, period! Looking in the mirror and liking what you see gets a lot easier when you believe you're worth it and that you matter. The curveballs of life can really present a challenge, and implementing even a few of the steps in this book will help you get one step closer to creating your own knockout image… stress free.

Creating a style all your own doesn't necessarily mean you dress for success every day, ready to turn heads. But it does mean that there's a healthy balance between the silent message your image conveys and the one you're intending to convey. Since you only have one chance to make a great first impression, putting some thought into your daily dressing routine can come with a big ROI. It doesn't matter if you're a stay-home mom, a work-from-home woman, or a corporate executive. You are missing opportunities and open doors if you don't take this principle to heart.

One of the chapters in my book, titled "Accessorize to Maximize," shares many examples of how you can invest an extra five minutes a day to create a "Dash out the Door" look with simple makeup techniques and fashion accessories to take every dressing dilemma and make it dynamic. No more frumpies…only fab-YOU-lous. Adding a chic scarf, a bling ring, and the right lip color, as well as having the right haircut that accents your face shape and clothing styles that flatter your figure are all guarantees that you'll be kissing the uglies goodbye and saying hello to a more beautiful you.

The real beauty is: others will notice too! Sometimes a quick fix on the outside perpetuates the transformation taking place on the inside, and often you just need a little help pulling out your inner beauty to reflect the true you. Since we start out naked every day, why not embrace the idea to pull together the best knockout package we can? Anybody can be ordinary, but with a little extra effort, your look can be extraordinary. Take those five minutes—you're worth it!

Wendy Lyn Phillips is an image expert, speaker, and bestselling author of *Naked to Knockout: Beauty from the Inside Out*. Her expertise has been featured in media across the country, and she is host of the TV show *Naked to Knockout*. Visit her official site at WendyLynOnline.com.

Beauty Solutions for the Stressed Out

There are hundreds of tips and ideas throughout this book to reduce stress. Implementing even just one or two will make a huge difference in your physical appearance. But there are some specific steps you can take to help protect your external assets. Give these a try for a more vibrant appearance *and* better health all around.

1. **Drink more water.** This is a universal rule that every health practitioner, fitness guru, nutritionist, or other wellness professional will tell you. Water helps your body run efficiently. It's like oil for your car. It makes all the parts run smoothly. Red blood cells have a lifespan of about 120 days, which means that your body is constantly producing fresh blood. A steady supply of water ensures that the blood cells you produce are pure and that they are suspended in the right chemical balance of constituents. I won't go biology teacher again on you, but let's just say that not drinking enough water turns your blood and body fluids to sludge, and that is not a good thing. Water also keeps your skin plump and hydrated, leading to a fresher, more youthful complexion. It keeps toxins from accumulating in the body and helps flush them out faster. And of course, it also helps to flush away those nasty stress chemicals that take up residence during challenging times. Aim for eight cups of water or more a day. After just a few days, you will notice your energy levels increase, your skin will become clearer and brighter, and you will just feel better.

2. **Up your moisturizer in winter and reduce in summer.** Your skin is the largest organ of your body. It lives and breathes as the first line of defense against negative influences in the environment. In the winter, cold air and lower humidity levels suck the moisture from skin, leaving it parched and less able to transport toxins out of you through perspiration. It needs a steady supply of water and moisture to keep it functioning

properly. In addition to drinking more water in the winter, switch your moisturizer to a more hydrating formula. In the summer, our skin gets oilier and doesn't need as much of the external hydration, so switch to a gel-based moisturizer or light lotion. But be sure to still drink tons of water to keep things fresh. Any department store can advise you on your skin type. And don't feel pressured to buy their products. Experiment until you find the right products for your skin, and when you find that magic combination, stick with it.

3. **Take vitamin D.** This crucial nutrient is often called the sunshine vitamin because our body naturally produces it when we are exposed to direct sunlight. Vitamin D has been linked not just to skin health, but to immunity, heart health, and better functioning of almost every body system. If you want to boost your immune system to help prevent those unsightly runny noses and other icky, ugly symptoms, try vitamin D. About ten minutes in direct midday sun with exposed arms and legs produces about 10,000 IU of vitamin D. The recommended daily allowance of vitamin D is only 400 IU, but most doctors are now recommending 1000 and up to 5000 IU per day of vitamin D, especially for those in northern climates, darker skinned individuals, and those who get little to no sun exposure. This simple addition to your daily routine can help you feel and look better within just a few days. Talk to your doc and try adding vitamin D to your stress relief plans.

4. **Wear sunscreen year round.** Stress can seriously damage skin and wreak havoc on your appearance. One line of defense to help protect skin and prevent compounding the damage being done is to wear sunscreen every single day. It protects your skin from the damaging rays of the sun, which can speed even further the sagging, wrinkling, discoloration, and general aging of your skin. Most skin experts recommend wearing

SPF15 or higher every single day. I wear an organic, inexpensive, nonchemical SPF every day, and it has made a huge difference in my skin. Experiment until you find one you like, and make it a regular part of your beauty routine. Guys should do this too!

5. **Get fresh air.** Breathing in fresh oxygen keeps your blood and body from becoming stagnant and toxic. If you can get outside regularly, keep your home well ventilated, have houseplants around, and learn to take deep breaths, you will get more oxygen naturally. That oxygen will feed your skin and body, boost your immune system, and keep you healthy. Now go ahead—breathe deep!

6. **Exercise.** Stress chemicals circulate and cause damage to your skin and overall appearance. But the more you exercise, the faster those chemicals will be worked out of your body. And the increase in body temperature and blood flow helps to keep the skin healthy and glowing. Get moving, get sweating, and feel the stress disappear while you look great.

Now What?

As you begin to change your habits and lifestyle, your physical appearance *will* change too. Over time your wrinkles will soften, your skin will get glow-y and clear, you'll get sick less often, and you will be motivated to pull yourself together when you go out in public because you'll feel so much better all around. But if you want to fast track your progress to becoming more attractive and downright H.O.T., then try some of the tips in this chapter to boost the already powerful stress-fighting tools that you choose to use from the rest of the book.

Three Keys to Simplifying Your Wardrobe Dilemmas

by Joyce Rosenblad, image consultant
and founder of Get Your Style On

Do you dread that morning ritual of picking out the perfect outfit for your day? Feel like you never know what to wear? In today's busy world, we often only get one chance to make that all-important first impression, so how do we choose pieces that not only look good on us but make us come across as authentic and believable?

We're all pressed for time in the morning, but by implementing these three easy tips, you will start your day off feeling fresh, confident, and ready to take on the world.

1. Choose pieces that feel in sync with your own energy.
When you put on a blouse, jacket, or dress, look closely in the mirror. Do you see yourself or do you see the item of clothing? If your eyes go directly to the clothing, chances are it is not in your element. You want people to notice *you*, not necessarily what you are wearing. By wearing clothing that *is* in your element, you will feel like yourself and people will naturally be drawn to you. As Coco Chanel put it, "With a good outfit, people will compliment the outfit. A great outfit, people will notice the woman."

2. Weed out your closet at least once a season.
Clothing should come with expiration dates. If it's stained, out of style, worn, poorly fitted, or simply doesn't look good on you, it's time to bid the garment adieu. Consign the best pieces and pack up the rest for your favorite charity. We wear 20 percent of our clothes 80 percent of the time, so keep your closet neat and organized by

color, with your favorite pieces displayed prominently. Otherwise, that fabulous cape you bought in Paris could end up in a ball at the back of your closet, forgotten until the next time you move!

3. Only buy clothing in your color palette.
This is the simplest but most difficult step to follow. When you build a wardrobe based on color harmonics that work for you, you can mix and match most of the pieces in your closet and create several outfits. You may choose to work with an image consultant for help in this area, but it will simplify your life and save you a lot of money over time—plus it makes shopping easy and fun!

Joyce Rosenblad is an image consultant, stylist, and wardrobe expert. For more ideas about simplifying your wardrobe, go to getyourstyleon.com.

Secret #8 STRESS UGLIES Action Grid				
Action Step	Guidelines	Time to Implement	Simple/ Medium/ Hard	Fun/ Easy/ Important
Smile	Open yourself up and give a grin at every chance you get. People will relate more positively to you, and you will just feel better.	Instant	S	FEI
Drink More Water	Staying hydrated is a key part of wellness *and* stress management. If your body isn't primed to function well, the inevitable stress that does come your way will be much harder to fight off, leading to illness, skin problems, and more. Aim for eight cups per day. Go fill up right now!	Instant	S	EI
Get Fresh Air	Oxygen is literally a lifesaver. It is required to survive, so be sure you're taking in fresh, clean air as often as possible. Your skin will look better and your body will function right. Take deep breaths regularly throughout the day, go outside for a quick walk, and open the window in your house regularly (even in winter).	Instant	S	FEI
Wear Sunscreen	Stress really does a number on your skin. Help protect it from even more damage by wearing sunscreen all year round, every single day. Go with at least an SPF of 15 and experiment to see if your skin responds better to nonchemical or chemical formulations, organic vs. nonorganic, etc. Skincare is serious stuff, but it can be fun too. Experiment to find your best products.	1 day	S	EI
Put Your Best Face Forward	Make the choice to put effort into your appearance every day. When you look good, you feel good. Take this seriously and your confidence will go up while your stress levels go down.	1 day	S	FEI
Exercise	When you exercise, you perspire, breathe faster, and up your blood circulation—all of which help to get stress chemicals out of your body faster. And the change in temperature and increased blood flow will make your skin glow! Start today. It's never too late.	1 day	M	FI
Take Vitamin D	Go out and get yourself some Vitamin D for better health, stronger immunity, and better skin. Any pharmacy, grocery store, or mass retailer will carry it. Check with your doctor before trying any new health supplements.	7 days	S	E
Be Stylish	Don't settle for mom jeans and a frumpy sweatshirt. Learn what looks great on you and wear it often. Find a trusted friend or store associate to help you find your fashion sense.	14 days	M	FI
Moisturize Right	Flexing your skincare regimen to the seasons and changing needs of your body is a key to beautiful skin. Up your moisture in the winter and go lighter in the summer. And stick with it. Overnight changes are rare, but over time, you will see the benefits.	30 days	S	E

Remember to use GOALS when deciding which ideas to try:
Gut-Checked: It feels right.
Obtainable: You can accomplish it in a reasonable amount of time with reasonable effort.
Actionable: You can take steps to making it happen right now.
Life-Oriented: It fits with your lifestyle right now. You have the support to make it happen.
Small Steps: The goal can be broken down into multiple, tiny steps.

Secret #9
Ohm Isn't for Sissies

The Power of Meditation for
Less Stress, Happiness, and Health

"Learn what you are, and be such." —Pindar

Resources:

Get downloadable worksheets and
tutorials for Secret #9
Meditation at:

HHESecrets.com

*Use your smartphone to scan the below
QR code to go there now.*

Benefits:

- More relaxed over time.
- Less stress as you master your emotions.
- More focused on your goals.
- More resilient to change and stress.
- More calm when annoyances occur.
- Less anxious about big events or changes in life.
- Better grasp of your own goals and dreams.
- More comfortable in your own skin.
- More confident in your decisions.
- Ability to remain calm in the face of crisis or drama.
- Ability to teach kids to relax.
- Less stressful environment.
- Increased ability to prioritize and make progress on tasks.

What's on Tap?

When I first started meditating, I was clueless. I had been given a little booklet on Buddhism and meditation by a woman I had met in a writing class. I was totally open to anything at that point. My husband had died about a year before, and I was on my self-discovery path. I thought, "Heck, it can't hurt." So I sat down cross-legged on my bed in the dark. I closed my eyes and began chanting the mantra the book outlined. I can't for the life of me remember it right now, but it was a string of Sanskrit words that meant something like *we are all one and connected.* I said it over and over for what I thought *had* to have been at least twenty minutes. I looked up and a measly two minutes had passed! How could that be? Only two minutes? I got up in disbelief, thinking there was no way I could do that for so long. Yet over the next few hours, I felt a little different—a little less agitated, a tiny bit more peaceful. Nothing major happened, but I did feel different. The next day I tried it again. I was determined to make it happen for twenty minutes. Once again, just a few minutes, in I snuck a look at the clock and was shocked time was passing so slowly again. But then it happened: I felt more relaxed and less anxious for the rest of the day. That sealed the deal for me. If just a couple of minutes of sitting quietly could have that much impact on my outlook and physical well-being, imagine what would happen once I actually made it to twenty minutes—or more!

Over the course of the next two years, I experimented, researched, and learned all I could about meditation. I am certainly not a master or guru, but I have seen the real benefits of it in my life, *and* I have taught my preschool-age daughter to use some of the techniques I have learned, so she can calm herself when she is upset or emotional. I am a true believer, and the thousands of studies out there further solidify the power of meditation for a happier, healthier, and less stressed life. But how can we get started when we've never meditated before? How can we fit meditation into our busy lives to help us become more focused, more relaxed, and less stressed? The Happy Hour Effect Secret #9 will give you the quickest ways to make meditation a part of your daily life. We will learn:

- What meditation is
- Why meditation helps with stress
- How to start meditating quickly and easily
- Simple meditations to use at work and at home
- Next steps

Even if you have never considered meditation before, this chapter will show you the benefits to making it a priority in your life. The power it has to make our lives happier, healthier, and less stressed makes it one of the most important tools you can use to live a more relaxing life.

What Is Meditation?

There are hundreds of ways to meditate, from strict practices that focus your thoughts on a single mantra to less structured ways of clearing your mind and relaxing your body. The common theme between them is that they all help you to consciously relax the body and mind to change your emotional, mental, and physical states so you can live happier and healthier lives. It can be used across so many situations; it's hard to argue against meditation. You may need to energize after a long day at work or calm down after an anger-induced argument with a spouse. Other times you may need to change your body's response to a packed schedule or overwhelming to-do list. Meditation can help you short-circuit the stress response to challenges in your life and get you back to a state of acceptance, calm, and happiness.

Imagine your body and all of its biological processes that occur, down to your very cells. Remember that stress response I explained earlier in the book? And remember all of that damage that can occur to our bodies and in our lives because of it? Well, cellular-level interactions that happen in your body can actually be shifted, simply by meditating. Now I'm not saying five minutes sitting quietly in a

Breathing Through Stress

by Shannon Henry

My life circumstances would lead you to believe that I embody the word *stress*. In the year 2000 I became pregnant after three miscarriages, lost my husband to suicide halfway through that pregnancy, sold my home by word of mouth, bought a home in another state in a weekend, moved thirteen thousand miles across country, settled in my new home August 4, had my son August 31, spent my thirty-seventh birthday learning my sister had been diagnosed with terminal cancer, and ended the year with pneumonia, which I had been walking around with for months. I'm still here thriving, and one of the reasons I believe this is the case is because I have some useful stress relievers.

Here are two ways I relieve stress: First, stress happens in the present, but it is often exacerbated by anticipation of difficulty or negative outcomes in the future. Keeping myself in the present and in the moment ensures that those future difficulties stay firmly entrenched in the future. I start by planting my feet firmly on the ground, trying to feel the four corners of my feet. I take a deep cleansing breath, imagining that breath traveling down my body all the way to my feet and into the ground. As I release the breath, I release through my nose and imagine my stress leaving my body with a big sigh as the breath is escaping. Again, this allows me to focus my attention on the here and now and opens space in my body, relaxes my muscles, and ensures that I don't physically take on the emotional stress.

In those moments when "just breathing" isn't enough, I turn on music I love, crank it up to a decibel that, as my mom would say, "Doesn't allow me to think straight," and I move. First, I let my whole body feel the rhythm, then my shoulders start to roll—my right shoulder followed by the left. My arms curl around my torso, led by my hands and fingers, gliding like water snakes, gracefully leaving only a slight ripple on the surface of the water. I close my eyes and allow the music to move through my body, unencumbered by my inhibition. This is not a dance for critical eyes; it is a dance for me, for joyous release. I dance with my children and play loud rhythmic music to help us feel our bodies and ground us when we would prefer to escape, zone out, and retreat. Feeling our feet move across the floor and the music move through our bodies connects us to one another, to our place in this world.

dark room will heal all that ails you. *But,* if you make meditation a part of your life on a daily basis, it can help you more effectively handle the challenges that life throws your way. It can help stop the stress response in its tracks. It can lower blood pressure. It can decrease your heart rate. It relaxes tense muscles. It improves the quality and quantity of sleep. It can change your reaction to stressors so that you don't fly off the handle, but instead, calmly and rationally respond in a way that will benefit you and your loved ones. Meditation is like therapy that works instantly. In fact, more and more traditional medical doctors are recommending mediation to their patients because of the tremendous difference it can make on health and wellness.

A Case for Meditation

When I was widowed at age thirty-one and left with an infant to raise on my own, my body revolted. I could not get myself back to a place of health or happiness because I was sucked into stress, self-pity, and sickness. I tried eating more healthfully. I tried exercise. I tried seeing a therapist. Nothing worked. But when I started meditating, my body and brain started to open up again. They started to respond to my attempts to heal. I had energy again. The food and exercise choices I was making finally began to nourish me instead of just run right through me. The world came into focus again as the fog in my brain started to lift. Instead of letting negative interactions at work push me over the edge, I learned to use my breath to calm the panic and anger response. Today, I can instantly shift my body and brain response when a challenge or annoyance strikes. That's not to say I don't sometimes get angry, sad, stressed, or overwhelmed. After all, I am human. But a jerk driver cutting me off in traffic doesn't send me into a frenzy anymore because I have learned to take a few deep breaths and focus my energy on releasing the angst right when it begins instead of letting it anger me for the rest of the day.

As I discovered the power of meditation in my own life, I knew I needed to teach my daughter to do it too. She was just a toddler at the time and just starting to talk. But after researching and taking classes on meditation, I learned that it's never too early to start. I taught her to take deep breaths when she is feeling overwhelmed or overcome by emotions. She knows that if something doesn't feel right in her body, she needs to relax and breathe deeply to release the pain or discomfort. When she is on the verge of a meltdown, I don't need to tell her to take deep breaths. She does it on her own now with miraculous results. Having meditation as a tool for raising a balanced kid has certainly made my life easier as a parent. (Ask me again in ten years how it's working out, when she's a teenager!)

My personal experience with meditation is just one story amongst millions of testaments to the power it can have on our lives. The world is filled with individuals, centers, and research facilities that prove the benefits of meditation. In fact, research has shown that the brains of people who meditate are chemically and physically different than those who don't—in a good way.

Why Does Meditation Help with Stress?

Our bodies are designed to operate in extreme conditions. We can tolerate hunger or thirst. We can endure a racing heart or high blood pressure. We can survive heartbreaking loss or debilitating stress. But when we operate under conditions like these for too long, our bodies *will* revolt through the appearance of disease and mood changes that can affect our relationships and productivity. Our bodies prefer consistency and order in their operations. Homeostasis is the medical term for that regularity and balance in our bodies. It is during homeostasis that we are best able to heal and grow. For example, when we don't drink enough water, our cells suffer and can't operate optimally. We need water to survive, build new cells, and run smoothly. As water becomes scarce, our body responds by signaling the brain that we need fluids. We drink a glass of water and our body gets back in balance as our cells are hydrated and shift back to being fully operational. This is the body maintaining homeostasis.

When challenges cause the stress response to kick in, we are pushed out of homeostasis. Stress chemicals cause an extreme environment in our bodies, including elevations in blood pressure, heart rate, perspiration, and respiration. Our muscles tense up. Our immune system grinds to a halt. As we are pushed further from that balanced, homeostatic state, the greater the damage will be and the more it will disrupt our lives. Meditation can help restore homeostasis. It can shift our muscles, breathing, and body systems back into balance so we are operating harmoniously, down to our very cells.

Imagine a time you were extremely stressed about something. Perhaps you had a bad day at work and the anxiety of the day lingered, causing you to lose sleep and wake up the next day still feeling stressed about something that happened in the past. You get annoyed or angry that it's bothering you so much and the stress response is perpetuated longer than it needs to be. You are causing your own imbalance by hanging onto tension, not getting enough sleep, and stressing about a past event. Meditation can help you to release emotions that can lead to stress. It can help your body to respond differently to the stresses that do arise. The more often we meditate, the more normalized we can keep our bodies so that the extremes are minimized and homeostasis is maintained.

How Can You Start Meditating?

With all of the research and case studies that promote meditation as a powerful stress reliever, it's clear that we need to take action to implement it into our lives. But if you're a newbie like I was just a couple of years ago, it can be confusing and even a little bit scary to sit with yourself—even for just a few minutes. Meditation forces us to get in touch with emotions, feelings, and past experiences that may not be pleasant. But it can also propel us forward so powerfully that we are able to make lasting and positive changes in our lives.

When getting started with meditation, the first thing to remember is that there is no right or wrong approach or way to do it. If all you can manage is thirty seconds of quiet time sitting on the toilet in the morning, that's a great first step! If you can't get your mind to settle down, that's okay too. There's a lot going on up there, and it's hard to harness it. Meditation is a practice because it requires exactly that—practice. Start slow. Start small. Here are some easy ways to begin exploring meditation while making it a part of your life:

- **Take a class.** When you're first getting started, you may want more personal instruction and interaction with a trained meditation guru. If this seems like an option you would like to try, go online and type in *meditation* along with your city name. Large cities will usually have several centers that offer meditation classes. Many community education programs also offer meditation classes. If you are in a smaller community, there may not be anything nearby. In that case, you will have to explore some of the options below to get started on your path, or take an online class. And remember, people of all walks of life meditate. You can be a Christian, Jew, Muslim, Buddhist, or a nonbeliever and still meditate. Don't be afraid to attend a meditation class or try it at home because you think it's only for a certain type of person or belief system.

- **Get an app.** This is my favorite option for finding meditations that can help you stay focused when you first get started. Simply go to the application store for whatever digital service provider you use (Droid, iPhone, etc.). Type in *meditation* and lists will come up with many variations of practice and teachers. Look at the ratings and read the descriptions until you find one or two that sound like they fit your needs. Some focus on stress. Others on sleep. Some just offer music. Others have subliminal messages embedded into them. The options are endless. And luckily, with the low cost of apps these days, you can download many for free or for just a dollar or two. It's a great way to experiment and find what works for you.

- **Listen to or watch.** There are thousands of online resources, CDs, and DVDs that can guide you as you enter the world of meditation. Just like apps above, you can search out resources in iTunes or online, and thousands of options will come up. Either purchase the product or download it to your computer or digital player to watch or listen at home, on the road, at work, or anywhere you have access to it. Don't be discouraged if the first few times are difficult or if you don't enjoy the process. Keep it up and experiment with different meditations until you find something that inspires you to keep doing it. Repetition is the key!

- **Just sit.** Meditation doesn't have to be a specific "program" or "system." It can simply be just sitting quietly and being present in the moment, wherever you are. You can even do it sitting in busy traffic or at your desk at work. Just get your mind focused on what is happening to you right at that moment. Become aware of your surroundings: the sounds, sights, smells, temperature—everything you can notice about where you are at that very second. If you can learn to do this several times throughout the day, you will find that you will feel more relaxed and better able to calm yourself down when stressful situations arise.

Getting Started

Meditation is as simple as just sitting for a few moments of quiet and self-reflection. It's also as difficult as trying to get a monkey to sit still for a few moments of quiet and self-reflection. The crazy wandering of our brain during meditation is often called monkey mind for that very reason. It wants to jump around from thought to thought. It wants to swing from idea to idea. It wants to nitpick and overanalyze. And yes—it can drive us bananas sometimes! I am cursed by an especially crazy monkey mind. It keeps me awake at night. It brims with seeds of invention that beg to be logged in one of my many idea notebooks.

Intuition and Stress Q & A

by Michael Mapes, psychic medium and speaker

Q: What is intuition?
Intuition is the way that you gain knowledge about a situation, circumstance, or person, making use of, but not requiring, reason. It is the way you get information about something in your life without the use of your normal five senses. Intuition is your "gut feelings" or the sense you get from *just knowing* that something is true. Intuition acts as an internal GPS. When you learn to listen to it, intuition guides you to your perfect destination.

There are countless stories of people thinking about someone moments before they call, waking up in the middle of the night at the exact moment their child is having a nightmare across town, or having a dream about someone they have never met only to encounter that exact person the next day. This is intuition.

Q: Who uses intuition?
Every person on the planet uses their intuition at some point. Even science is teaching us that we all have the capacity to use our intuition to improve our lives. Today you are just as likely to find a corporate recruiter talking about listening to her intuition when selecting candidates for a job as you are a local gypsy with her neon sign advertising "psychic readings." Even some Olympic athletes are known to consult their intuition before they compete, as a way of trying to get information about circumstances that are outside of their control.

Q: How can intuition reduce stress?
Your intuition acts as an early warning system that can help you

avoid stressful situations. The adage *knowledge is power* applies here. We tend to experience less stress about situations in which we feel empowered, and intuition helps empower you by gifting you with all the knowledge you need to make good decisions.

Most of us are receiving information from our intuition all the time—we have just been conditioned not to listen to it. We interview for a job, feel like it is not a good fit, take the job anyway, and find ourselves miserable six months later. Or we lend money to a friend, even when our gut tells us not to, and never get paid back. Imagine how different things would have been in these examples if you had listened to your intuition.

Q: How do I listen to my intuition?
Learn to pay attention to your first impression. These impressions are powerful because your mind does not yet have enough information to make a decision based on reason, so your intuitive sense kicks in to guide you. Get in the habit of asking for intuitive information when faced with a big decision, and note what you feel. You may want to get in the habit of writing down these impressions so you can remember and refer to them later. The more you practice working with your intuition the easier it will get. Ultimately, the best decisions are those that make use of both intuition and emotion, as well as logic and reason.

At the age of five, Michael declared to his preschool teacher that he was psychic. Since that time, he has read for people on every continent, traveled the United States talking about spirituality and intuition, and participated in scientific research designed to test his abilities as a medium. Michael regularly appears at spiritual expos and holistic fairs as a workshop leader and panelist, as a guest speaker at Unity and New Age churches, and on various radio programs. Michael's focus on the practical application of spirituality is aimed at helping the busy spiritual seeker create meaning and purpose in their lives. His official site is MichaelMapes.org.

I love my monkey mind, but I also know there are times I need to shut it off—especially at bedtime or during times of stress or sickness. During those times in life, we need to nurture and pamper our bodies and brains and help them get back to that place of homeostasis. Meditation can help us do this by allowing the thoughts to still arise, but then letting them go instead of dwelling on them or allowing them to propel us down a rabbit hole. The basics to getting started are pretty common, regardless of the type of meditation you actually engage in.

1. **Get situated.** Meditation can be done sitting, standing, lying down, or anywhere you can focus on the present moment and relaxation. You can do it for just a couple of minutes or spend weeks at a meditation retreat. I like to sit on a chair or exercise ball, but you can sit on a pillow or mat on the floor, sit at your desk, or even sit in your car. (Obviously you won't be closing your eyes while driving.) The key is to get yourself into a position where you can really focus on the present moment and what is happening in the *now*. If you are at home sitting on the floor, you can close your eyes and rest your hands on your lap. Or you can keep your eyes open and just breathe deeply. It's up to you to decide what feels the most comfortable. I simply sit on a chair, close my eyes, and then start to focus.

2. **Find your focus.** Many people have an image, mantra, or other item to focus on during meditation. Simply stare or repeat your focus over and over again as you breathe deeply and slowly, letting your thoughts recede. It can be breath or a part of the body that you concentrate on during your meditation session. It can be a special figurine or piece of artwork placed in front of you, or an image you keep in your mind. I don't recommend you use a photo or image of a person because of the emotions that are tied to individuals. Instead, choose an inanimate object that empowers or calms you. I usually use a mantra to keep me on track. A mantra is a phrase or keyword that you repeat over and over to keep your mind from wan-

dering. This phrase or word can be something personal to you or even just a random word. I often use *there is enough time for everything* during my meditations because much of my stress comes from a big to-do list. Other times I use the word *evolve* because it reminds me to be flexible and change with the times instead of getting stuck. I don't necessarily think about that while I meditate, but the word is there to be repeated and keep me focused. You can choose any word or phrase that inspires you. Here are some examples of mantras you can use. Try one or all of them, or create your own.

- Peace.
- Joy.
- I am calm.
- I am in control of me.
- Let it go.
- I am lucky because_____.
- We are all connected.
- Love.
- Relax.
- I have composure.
- I control my destiny.
- I can help the world.
- I am free to be myself.
- Slow down.
- Nothing is permanent.
- Change is good.
- Faith.
- I am strong.

As you repeat the mantra—visual or breath over and over—concentrate on your breath filling you up and your body systems responding by relaxing with every inhale and exhale. I like to envision myself breathing in positivity with each inhale and breathing out negative energy with every exhale. But you will find your own patterns as you develop your practice. The goal is to begin to connect the act of focusing on your mantra—visual or breath—with the relaxation of your body. You are slowly conditioning yourself to relax simply by repeating your focus. I have gotten to the point that when a situation arises that makes me angry or anxious, I can simply take a couple of deep breaths and repeat *evolve* to myself a couple of times and my body naturally calms down as my brain also relaxes. It's quite amazing!

3. **Refocus.** As you focus on your mantra, try to stay focused on it. Other thoughts will try to creep in and take over. That's okay. Let them come, take note of them, and then let them go as you refocus. This will be the bulk of your practice—constantly refocusing as thoughts arise. Remember that thinking is okay, but the goal is to get your brain and body to a place of relaxation and present awareness. You don't want to let thoughts of the past or the future sneak in and overtake your meditation practice. You want to train your brain to focus on the here and now. This means that when you are sitting in meditation, you will have to force yourself to stop analyzing, to stop second-guessing, and to stop judging. It will be difficult and will take time, but it will pay off big time in your health, happiness, and ability to deal with stress. Make meditation a priority in your life.

4. **Let go.** As simple as meditation sounds, it isn't. It is hard work, but it's powerful work. It needs to occur in your life to take you to a higher level of health, happiness, and connection. But you must let go of expectations. You will not master it overnight. It will take time. It will feel weird. You will think you don't have time for it. But if you make a commitment to it, it will make a difference in more ways than you ever imagined. But you must let go of what you think it should be and just let it be. The more often you do it, the easier it will be-

come. The more open you are to experimenting and learning about meditation, the faster it will work. Let go of all of the preconceived notions of what, who, and how meditation is and it can become a powerful tool for stress relief, long-term health, and abundant happiness.

Now What?

Meditation is not daydreaming. It isn't passively sitting quietly. Meditation is a practice that requires hard work, patience, and commitment. It won't work if you don't believe in it. But you don't have to take my word for it. The biggest universities and research institutions in the world have researched the benefits of meditation, so do your own research to discover how meditation can help you elevate your life in ways you never would have imagined. If you start slowly, it will change your life for the better just like it has for me and millions of others across the world. Use these simple tips to get started on a path to less stress through meditation.

Get Present with Meditation

by Tom Von Deck, meditation trainer, speaker, and author

Meditation is the art of being present with moment-to-moment experience instead of simply reacting to it. We tend to push away uncomfortable experience and embrace the familiar and comfortable. This attraction and repulsion process creates most of our baggage and entanglements. When you watch the thoughts, emotions, and sensations in each moment, it becomes easier to see every situation in perspective.

Meditation has many factors that contribute to stress relief, one already mentioned directly above. Another is increased oxygen flow. Yet another is the generation of synapses connecting the neurons of the brain. This brings a more efficient and stronger flow of communication between the various parts of the brain.

To really optimize the benefits of meditation, you need to accumulate peace with a consistent momentum. Meditation is not a sporadic exercise. Each session builds on the next. That is why many people do a formal practice at the same time each day. The habit building is the single biggest factor in a successful meditation technique.

There are many different tricks you can use to make meditation easier. One is a warm-up program of stretching, deep breathing, prayer, gratitude, or anything else that helps you center. You can also take all these calming exercises and integrate them into your day for a stronger momentum of peace. Spend at least thirty seconds out of each hour centering yourself in some way. The peace will accumulate to the point where meditation becomes a much easier process.

Tom Von Deck is a corporate meditation trainer, speaker, and author of *Oceanic Mind: The Deeper Meditation Training Course*. Tom specializes in making meditation easier for busy people from all cultural and religious backgrounds. His website is deepermeditation.net.

Secret #9 MEDITATION Action Grid

Action Step	Guidelines	Time to Implement	Simple/ Medium/ Hard	Fun/ Easy/ Important
Just Sit	The easiest way to start meditating is to just sit. It's harder than you think. Just stop what you're doing right now and focus on this moment. Don't think about what happened yesterday or what you have to do an hour from now. Just stop. Just sit. Just breathe. Just be.	Instant	S	FEI
Have an Open Mind	Meditation is practiced by every culture, religion, and demographic across the world. It is truly for everyone, and research shows that it can benefit everyone in so many ways. Just give it a try.	Instant	S	—
Try a Mantra	If your mind won't stop spinning, try a mantra to keep yourself focused. It can be a short saying like, "Breathe," or it can be staring at an object placed a few feet in front of you just below eye level. Experiment.	1 day	S	FEI
Get an App	If you type "meditation" into your mobile device's app store, hundreds of options will come up—some free, some paid. Give them a try and see if any feel right for you.	1 day	S	FE
Take a Class	Go online or search newspapers or community education mailers for classes that can get you started. Many communities have spiritual or wellness centers that offer classes.	7 days	M	FE
Research and Read	Go online or to the library or bookstore to learn about the different kinds of meditation and how to get started.	7 days	S	EI
Learn How	There is no right or wrong way to meditate, but having some guidance to get you started will keep you motivated.	7 days	M	—
Be Patient	Don't expect miraculous changes overnight. Even lifetime meditators report struggling with monkey mind and staying focused. Just build in time to sit quietly every single day, even if it's just for a few minutes. Over time you will feel less agitated and more grounded.	30 days	H	—

Remember to use GOALS when deciding which ideas to try:
Gut-Checked: It feels right.
Obtainable: You can accomplish it in a reasonable amount of time with reasonable effort.
Actionable: You can take steps to making it happen right now.
Life-Oriented: It fits with your lifestyle right now. You have the support to make it happen.
Small Steps: The goal can be broken down into multiple, tiny steps.

Resources:

Get downloadable worksheets and
tutorials for Secret #10
Hair, Poop, and Feedings at:

HHESecrets.com

*Use your smartphone to scan the below
QR code to go there now.*

Benefits:

- Nonstop entertainment from your animal friends.
- Unconditional love from your animal friends.
- You will find yourself with a more relaxed demeanor after spending time with animals.
- New options for entertainment, like zoos, museums, aquariums, and farms.
- More appreciation for nature and animal life.
- Higher connection to the world around you.
- Teach kids responsibility in taking care of a pet.
- Teach kids respect of other living things.
- Lots of smiles and cuddles with your animal friends = increased happiness and less stress.

Secret #10
Hair, Poop, and Feedings: Sounds Stressful to Me!

How Owning a Pet Can
Reduce Stress and Elevate Happiness

"Animals are such agreeable friends—they ask no questions,
they pass no criticisms." —George Eliot

What's on Tap?

Owning a pet is a labor of love. The hair, poop, feedings, and attention can feel like a huge job sometimes. I own a giant black Lab named Cosmo, and there are days when I curse the fact that I'm an animal lover. But when it comes down to it, the relationship with him—the unconditional love, the entertainment, and the external focus on another living being—greatly outweighs all the hassles of pet ownership.

By the time this book is published, Cosmo won't be with me anymore. He has bone cancer that will only give him another few months at most. The idea of losing him is heartbreaking. The pitter patter of his feet, his soft breathing at the foot of the bed each night, and the excited wagging of his tail every time I get home are things that I can't imagine living without. The emotions and sadness over losing him are proof-positive that owning him was worth it. He gave me something special in the years he's been with me. He filled my heart and home with love and happiness. That is what pets can do for us. They can add a dimension to our lives that changes how we view the world. And in this relationship, we become happier, more connected, and healthier overall.

There is extensive research that shows that animals can be a very powerful part of our lives. Some studies show that pet owners are actually happier, healthier, and recover from illness faster. So how can we make more time to connect with pets and animals as part of our daily life? How can we maximize our animal relationships and use them to feel connected to the world in a bigger way? The Happy Hour Effect Secret #10 will reveal fun and relaxing ways to spend more time with pets and animal life to help us stress less. We will learn:

- Ways to integrate animals into your life
- How kids can benefit from animals
- Next steps

Whether you're a pet owner or just an animal lover, or even if you haven't spent much time with animals, you can find ways to use your relationship with them in a way that can make you happier, healthier, and less stressed. Open your mind to the benefits that quality time with animals can bring and you will find it to be a fulfilling, relaxing, and powerful tool to minimize your stress and maximize your life.

Pets and Stress

How many times have you been sucked into an animal rescue TV show or found yourself enthralled by that pacing tiger at the zoo? There is just something about seeing another living creature living its life and going about its business. Animals are a part of life for people across the globe. The most remote tribes in Africa have wildlife around them. People living in the tiniest studio apartments in the biggest cities in the world make room for pets.

There are so many ways you can spend time with animals, whether it's as a pet owner or just making it a priority to appreciate them in other environments outside your own home.

- **Get a pet.** People who own pets are generally healthier, happier, and may even live longer. If you're able and up for the responsibility, get yourself a furry, feathered, or finned friend.

- **Borrow a pet.** If your circumstances— like allergies, apartment rules, or just not wanting the responsibility—don't allow you to have a pet, make it a point to spend time with the pets of your friends and family.

- **Go to a zoo.** I'll be honest: I have a love-hate relationship with zoos. I hate seeing animals trapped in unnatural surroundings, yet I know that many have been rescued and wouldn't survive in the wild. And it is fun to see animals close up and watch their behaviors.

- **Go to an aquarium.** Like a zoo, aquariums give you a chance to see nature close up. They are fun, and watching underwater worlds can be very meditative.

- **Volunteer at a shelter.** Doing good for someone or something else can boost your feel-good chemicals, *and* it's a double boost when you're spending time with animals.

- **Make your yard animal-friendly.** Animals are all around us. On a recent trip to Disney's Animal Kingdom with my daughter, there was an exhibit showing a small patio like any of us might have. It gave several ways to make it attractive to all kinds of animals.

- **Take a walk in nature.** This one is so easy. Simply go outside, walk, and look around. Chances are you'll spot a rabbit hidden under a bush or an ant crawling on the ground. If you're feeling adventurous, hit your closest park or nature trails and go for a hike.

- **Watch animal TV shows.** This may sound silly, but I bet you have found yourself sucked into *Animal Planet* or *America's Funniest Home Videos* at least once because of some silly cat running in circles or a dopey dog doing something adorable. YouTube has millions of funny animal videos, so go online and watch.

- **Support animal rescue organizations.** If you can't spend time in the physical presence of animals, support charities that help protect and rescue wildlife and pets.

Teaching Kids About Animals

Kids love animals. My daughter will watch ants working for hours or track a caterpillar across the patio to be sure he gets to the grass safely. Imagine her glee at owning her own pets and caring for them every single day! Not only is she finding joy in her animal interactions, but it teaches her to respect other creatures. Plus, as she gets older, I am giving her more of the caretaking tasks, which teaches her responsibility. She loves to feed her fish every day. She knows that we can't feed them too much or their tummies will get too big and they will die. She knows to give the dog one-and-a-half cups of food for his mealtimes and that we shouldn't give him too many table scraps or he could get sick. Exposing kids to animals can help them appreciate nature and build their connection to other living beings. In the long run, this will help them become more caring and happier adults—and of course, being with animals will help them stress less too!

Now What?

Spending time with animals is one of my favorite ways to reduce stress. Plus, it's so easy to find a spot of nature almost anywhere on the planet. Try these action steps we discussed throughout the chapter and you'll be benefitting yourself and your animal friends too.

Pets and Stress Reduction

by Darlene Arden, C.A.B.C.,
animal expert and award-winning author

Decades ago, Drs. Alan Beck and Aaron Katcher's groundbreaking research showed that talking about pets or stroking a pet's fur would lower blood pressure. Today, more researchers have shown further proof of the benefits of pets when it comes to stress and the human body.

According to a recent study, a cat companion reduces your risk of stroke or heart disease by about 30 percent. It is known that the purring of a cat not only heals the cat but also the owner because of the decibels at which it reverberates.

Playing with or training your dog or cat (yes, cats can be trained) will help you relax and reduce your stress levels. Walking a dog isn't just good exercise—it's a good time to relax and unwind with your four-legged friend. De-stressing was never so easy. *Heel* and *heal* aren't that far apart in this case.

Dog and cat agility, canine musical freestyle, Rally-O, and Frisbee are just a few of the sports you and your pet can play that will get you away from everyday worries, introduce you to more people, and channel your energy into fun and rewarding games that will help reduce stress and help you unwind.

Pets aren't for everyone, but if you have time and can afford a pet, that relationship will pay priceless dividends in stress reduction.

Darlene Arden, an award-winning writer, lecturer, and author of *The Irrepressible Toy Dog* (Howell Book House) and *The Angell Memorial Animal Hospital Book of Wellness and Preventive Care for Dogs* (Contemporary Books) is an internationally recognized authority on toy dogs and their care. She is also a certified animal behavior consultant and has written hundreds of articles and columns for all of the major dog and cat publications, as well as for newspapers and general interest publications. Visit her official site at DarleneArden.com.

Secret #10 PETS Action Grid

Action Step	Guidelines	Time to Implement	Simple/ Medium/ Hard	Fun/ Easy/ Important
Take a Walk	This is simple and easy—plus you are getting exercise too. As you walk, notice the birds, insects, and other living creatures you encounter along the way.	1 hour	S	FEI
Watch Animal TV Shows	If all else fails, turn on the TV and tune in to one of the many programs about wildlife and pets. But don't get sucked into the TV for too long—in-person animal experiences are better.	1 hour	S	FE
Support Animal Charities	When you look at the charities you support, build in room for one that helps animals. It could protect endangered species or help rescue abandoned pets. Whatever it is, you are helping animals in a powerful way.	1 hour	S	EI
Borrow a Pet	When pet ownership isn't for you, borrow a friend's pet and go for a walk. Or offer to pet sit when they are out of town.	1 day	M	F
Go to the Zoo	A quick and fun way to interact with animals is at the zoo. Spend a day there and really observe animals and their habits.	1 day	S	FE
Go to an Aquarium	Aquariums are fascinating and peaceful. The underwater world is so silent and calm. And watching animal life swim and live in this watery environment can be entertaining and enlightening too.	1 day	S	FE
Include Kids	Don't forget the importance of educating kids on animals. Teach them to respect animals. Teach them the responsibility of owning and caring for a pet.	1 day	S	FEI
Volunteer at a Shelter	You can help animals and help society by volunteering your time at a shelter. Those animals are in desperate need of love and attention—a perfect opportunity for you to give some.	7 days	M	FI
Create an Animal-Friendly Yard	Even a caterpillar inching across a patio can be an enthralling and enriching experience. Look around you and find ways to bring nature into your backyard. Add plants. Get a birdfeeder.	14 days	M	F
Get a Pet	This can be the most gratifying way to spend time with an animal. You develop a relationship of unconditional love, and you are responsible for taking care of the pet for its entire life. It's a lot of work, but it's well worth it if you foster the relationship.	30 days	H	FI

Remember to use GOALS when deciding which ideas to try:

Gut-Checked: It feels right.

Obtainable: You can accomplish it in a reasonable amount of time with reasonable effort.

Actionable: You can take steps to making it happen right now.

Life-Oriented: It fits with your lifestyle right now. You have the support to make it happen.

Small Steps: The goal can be broken down into multiple, tiny steps.

V.
Dreams

Secret #11
Me-Time for Less Stress

Okay, I'm Alone. Now What?

"I never found the companion that was so
companionable as solitude." —Henry David Thoreau

Resources:
Get downloadable worksheets and
tutorials for Secret #11
Me-Time at:

HHESecrets.com

*Use your smartphone to scan the below
QR code to go there now.*

Benefits:
- Faster progress toward goals.
- Reduced stress levels.
- Clearer decision making.
- Better parenting.
- More respectful
  relationships.
- Boost in feel-good chemicals
  in the body.
- More fulfilling life.
- Greater perspective on life.
- More empathetic to others.
- Great role model for kids.
- More independent children.
- Stronger ability to move
  forward during challenge.
- More resilient to change.

What's on Tap?

When was the last time you had a full day to yourself and you spent it truly alone? Not just a trip to the grocery store. I'm talking a time it was just you doing what you wanted to do with your time and energy all day long. Most people I meet can't remember the last time they had any real me-time beyond a quick trip to the spa or trip to the mall.

When I remind clients to take a few hours to themselves doing exactly what they want to do, the reports I get back are astounding. They feel more energetic, happier, healthier, and yes, less stressed! And yet, despite these positive outcomes, most of us are still not taking the time we need and deserve to get in touch with ourselves on our own terms. Maybe it's mommy or daddy guilt. Maybe it's crazy schedules. Maybe it's that we aren't sure what to do with this me-time.

The Happy Hour Effect Secret #11 will help us to harness the spirit of self-development so our me-time rises to the top for our health, happiness, and stress levels. We will cover:

- Why me-time is so important
- Releasing guilt
- Carving out time
- Ideas for me-time
- Next steps

With just a few small changes to your schedule, you can find ways to build in more time for yourself for your own well-being and for the benefit of your loved ones.

Why Me-Time Is So Important

If someone asks you who you are, how do you answer? Most of us say something like, "I'm Kristen Brown. I live in Minneapolis with my five-year-old daughter. I'm a writer and own a company called Happy Hour Effect." It's an accurate description of my vital statistics, but it doesn't really explain *who* I am. If I answered the question the right way, I might say, "I'm a driven, passionate woman who has overcome some big challenges but found a way to rise above them. I love to inspire others to greatness and am fulfilled by spending time eating, boating, and traveling with my family, friends, and animals. I don't judge others' choices but provide perspective. I am grateful for every day I have on earth and am determined to leave a legacy that my daughter and the world can learn from and follow in their own lives." Okay, that got a little deep, but that is really who I am. The basics, like address and job, are just temporary facts that could change at any time.

But how do we get to a point of knowing who we are down to our very core? If you had asked me five years ago who I am, I would have rattled off the basics. But because I have spent so much time on my own really figuring out what I want and getting comfortable in my own skin, I am able to give you the true essence of myself in just a few sentences without having to think too hard. I've done the self-development work that has brought me to this place of complete satisfaction with my own choices and life.

That doesn't mean that every time I have some alone time I'm analyzing myself and working on improving my life. Sometimes I just lie on the couch while watching TV. Sometimes I hit the mall and buy impractical shoes and hit the food court. But even these simple outings alone give you time to make choices that are just for you. When I hit the mall alone, I can go into any stores I want. If I go to the grocery store, I can shop at my leisure and buy what I know will nourish me—instead of being persuaded to buy junky cereal that my daughter would pick out. And yes, I'm always considering my daughter in my decisions. But not having her right next to me every minute of the day gives us both the breathing room we need to figure out who we are and what our next move is going to be.

It's the same with a spouse, friends, or other family members. It's so important to have your own lives. When you have a life that you have created for yourself that includes *your* favorite hobbies and passions, you will be happier, less stressed, and one step closer to knowing who *you* are deep down to your very soul.

Releasing Guilt

One of the most common excuses I hear from people for not taking time for themselves is that they feel guilty for leaving their kids or significant other. Carly was a young mom who had a new baby and was back at work full-time. She was frazzled as she learned to balance all of her responsibilities as a new parent and working mom. As we looked at her to-do list and calendar, I asked her when she was taking time out for herself. She looked at me with her tired eyes and explained that she felt guilty leaving her baby at daycare all day and only having a couple of hours at night and the weekend to see him. She didn't feel like it was the right decision to leave him. I asked if her husband could watch him for a couple of hours one night per week so she could get some solo time in. She said she felt just as guilty asking her husband to watch the baby when he worked hard all day too. Yet he was spending substantial amounts of time with his friends for sports leagues and outings. I can't tell you how many times I've heard this same story.

Mommy and daddy guilt is easily one of the top reasons I hear for people not spending time doing things they enjoy just for themselves. But when I explain the detrimental effects of *not* taking me-time, the person is usually shifted pretty quickly into a new way of thinking and acting. So why should you take me-time?

- **Breathing room.** When you step away from your responsibilities for even just a couple of hours, your brain and body are given a chance to slow down and catch up. It's a little break in the middle of your busy, crazy life. It gives those nasty stress chemicals a chance to subside for a while.

- **Fun.** If you make a commitment to spend some time every week doing something you love to do just for *you*, it will add a spark of fun to life. When you do something fun that makes

Mastering the Art of Wholeness

by Lauren Mackler, bestselling author and coach

Many people spend years waiting for a soul mate to make them feel complete. Others settle for unfulfilling relationships out of fear of being alone. Instead of expecting someone else to complete you, mastering the art of wholeness gives you mastery of your own life. Here are six steps you can take to strengthen your relationship with yourself and develop greater self-esteem, personal fulfillment, and financial security on your own or in a relationship:

1. **Become self-sufficient.** Self-sufficiency builds self-esteem and confidence, allowing you to participate in relationships out of *conscious choice* instead of a *desperate need.* Identify the things in your life for which you are dependent on someone else (finances, emotional well-being, household tasks, etc.). Pick one and start taking responsibility for managing this for yourself.

2. **Live life by *deliberation* versus by *default.*** Instead of living on autopilot, align your behaviors and actions with the results you want to achieve. Before you react to a person or situation, stop and think about what you want to have happen. Once you've imagined your desired outcome, choose the action or behavior that's most likely to achieve it.

3. **Manage fear so it doesn't manage you.** Most fears are rooted in old beliefs adopted in childhood. When fear arises, write down what you're afraid will happen. Next, do a reality check to see if your fear is grounded in reality or based on a limiting belief. Replace limiting beliefs with self-supporting

ones that are based on your current reality, and that will lessen your fear so you can move forward.

4. **Become the partner you seek.** Instead of waiting for someone else to transform you, develop the attributes you'd want in a partner in yourself. Make a list of the qualities of your ideal mate, then circle those that are *not currently true about you.* Identify steps for developing the qualities you circled, then implement a plan of action.

5. **Take financial control.** Debt or scarce financial resources creates stress or dependency on others. Make a list of your monthly expenses and income. If you live beyond your means, you need to alter your lifestyle or develop an action plan for earning the money to support it.

6. **Do the work you were born to do.** The smaller the gap between who you are in your personal life and who you are at work, the happier you will be. Make a list of your strengths, skills, and passions, and brainstorm ways to turn them into a job or business. If you're not sure how to translate your strengths into a new career, hiring a career coach can help.

Lauren Mackler is a world-renowned coach, creator of the Illumineering method, and author of the international bestseller *Solemate: Master the Art of Aloneness and Transform Your Life.* Visit her official site at: LaurenMackler.com you happy, it stimulates the release of endorphins and other feel-good chemicals that boost your mood and help to counteract stress.

- **Positive role model.** When kids see that their parents are happy and secure in their own identities, they will grow up valuing that same mindset. They learn from you!

- **Kids forge new relationships.** When you leave your kids with other caregivers (spouse, babysitters, family, daycare providers), you are giving them the opportunity to learn how to develop new relationships with people. They are learning how to interact with diverse personalities and environments. This sense of independence and self-development is very important for kids as they grow up into adults.

- **Stronger relationship.** By developing the security in yourself on your own and allowing your spouse or significant other to do the same, you will both feel happier, less stressed, and more connected to each other because you are respecting your need for independence.

- **Decision making.** When you have time alone to reflect on big and small life changes and decisions, you are able to more clearly choose the path that is right for you and your loved ones. You don't have someone else swaying you to act one way or another.

If you start small, you can make me-time a priority and use it for a happier and less stressful life.

Releasing Fear

Another common reason for not indulging in time alone is fear. Most of us won't admit it, but the idea of trying new things on our own is terrifying. We want a support system to buffer the potential negative reactions we may get if we fail. *Will people look at me and think I'm a loser for being by myself? Will people think no one wants to be with me and then not like me because of it? What if it's too hard or I can't do it and there is no one there to catch me when I fall?* All kinds of self-judgment and self-doubt will creep in when we stretch ourselves to try new things—especially when we're alone in our new endeavors. Here are a few tips for releasing that fear and gathering the courage to make the leap to solo outings:

- **No one is looking at you.** Initially they may glance at you when you enter a room, but then they will be sucked back into their own little world again.

- **No one cares as much as you think they do.** If you are alone trying new things, focus on that instead of what you think others will think of you. Most people will either not take notice at all or be impressed by your ability to try new things.

- **Ignore naysayers.** When I first started to indulge in quality me-time, I had people who asked me how I could be away from my daughter or if I felt guilty. The simple answer was always, "No. I am a better parent and person by taking a little time for myself."

- **It's the old air mask example.** On an airplane they tell you in case of emergency to put on your own air mask first before assisting others. That is because they know that only if you take care of yourself first can you effectively take care of others. So put on your own air mask and start taking time for yourself.

As you begin to venture out into the world on your own, be brave. Don't be afraid of other people's judgments, of failure, or of letting yourself or others down. The goal of a time-out is to make you a happier, healthier, and less stressed person for yourself *and* for your loved ones. Always let that be your guiding force in the choices you make.

Carving out Time

Another common reason for denying ourselves the much needed me-time we deserve is our lack of time. We are so busy shuttling kids, working, running errands, and keeping up with household chores that even an hour of time alone seems impossible most days. But if we want to make progress toward a more peaceful and less stressful life, we must make it a priority and learn to shuffle our schedules to make it happen. The first and easiest step to start realigning your priorities with your goals is to read the Prioritization and GOALS chapters in this book. They outline specific ways you can start to free up time and energy by focusing on areas that energize you and areas that stress you the most. As you begin to shift things around in your life and start to make stress management and wellness a priority, your to-do lists and schedules will begin to fall into place too. The key is to start small. Even a couple of minutes a day is a great way to get used to spending time on your own doing exactly what you want for reasons that are just for you.

Ideas for Me-Time

Any hobby or passion that you have is a perfect way to spend your me-time. If it's been a while since you did something just for yourself, you may need to experiment for a while to figure out what you like to do. Here is a list of ideas to get you started:

- Pedicure/manicure
- Massage/spa day
- Movie (This is one of my favorites! Popcorn all to yourself and you can pick any movie you want!)
- Bookstore/library

- Picnic (Yes, a solo picnic in the park or at the beach can be super relaxing.)
- Take a class (exercise, knitting, language, meditation, cooking, scrapbooking, etc.)
- Volunteer
- Vacation (Solo travel is scary but well worth it!)
- Writing
- Shopping
- Retreats (yoga, writing, service trips, etc.)
- Gardening
- Restaurant/cafe (bring a book for company)
- Catch up on Tivo (sometimes we just need a veg out day!)

Now What?

Me-time is one of the easiest and quickest ways to start stressing less. Yet it is one of the most difficult to get people started with because of the guilt, time challenges, and fear that goes along with it. By starting with small chunks of time alone and building up to longer periods of self-reflection and activity, you will be putting into place a very powerful tool for health, happiness, and less stress.

Friendship Heals

by Barb Greenberg, author and advisor

On a Friday night at the beginning of August, I went to the Carver County Fair with three friends, each of us silently carrying a stressful assortment of financial and health issues. We were quite a group.

One of us had trouble walking, one had trouble hearing, and I had trouble staying awake. Luckily the youngest was in great shape and kept us moving.

We ate. We looked at horses, cows, goats, and sheep. We ate. We looked at beautiful floral arrangements and colorful quilts. We ate. And we laughed and laughed.

When it comes to relieving stress, we hear a lot about self care. We are instructed to eat well, exercise, get enough sleep, and keep our attitudes positive so we can move forward. There seems to be such a rush to move forward, and sometimes it seems like simply too much work.

Instead of moving forward, Friday night felt like going back in time and remembering the fairs we had attended when we were younger, how we loved horses, and how we used to be able to eat much more before our stomachs got upset. At the end of the evening I was calmer, more hopeful, more lighthearted, and more trusting that there is still so much joy to be found in life.

Sometimes we focus too much on work and on the practical pieces of life. And then dear friends come along and bring us out into the world—to fairs, on boat rides, and to shopping adventures. Their presence in our lives give us energy, confidence, and encouragement, and is also a powerful form of healing stress.

Barb Greenberg is an author, speaker, and businesswoman who offers support for women in transition, especially those dealing with divorce. Her books *Hope Grew Round Me* and *After the Ball: A Woman's Tale of Reclaiming Happily Ever After* are available exclusively at RosePathPress.com. Visit Barb's official site at BarbGreenberg.com.

Secret #11 ME TIME Action Grid

Action Step	Guidelines	Time to Implement	Simple/ Medium/ Hard	Fun/ Easy/ Important
Be Open-Minded	Don't let others make you feel guilty for spending time on your own. And be open-minded about trying it.	Instant	S	FEI
Get Out of the House	When you find yourself with a couple of free hours, don't just stay home and catch up on housework. Get out and explore the world.	1 hour	S	FEI
Don't Run Errands	Use your free time to do things you enjoy, like hobbies and new experiences. You can do errands with the kids or delegate them to your spouse. Instead, take your me-time seriously and do something just for yourself.	1 hour	S	FEI
Find Time	Schedule time on your calendar for your own hobbies and downtime. Stick to it and don't let other activities overtake your precious time.	1 day	M	FI
Experiment	Try new things. Get out of your comfort zone.	7 days	S	FEI
Let Go of Guilt	Kids and adults need time on their own to develop relationships with others. Time apart is not a bad thing as you're both spending the time learning and creating a happier you.	30 days	H	—
Release Fear	If you're not used to spending time alone, me-time can be scary. But remember that you are in control of your actions and very few, if any, people are taking notice of your activities. Just get out there and be brave!	30 days	H	—

Remember to use GOALS when deciding which ideas to try:

Gut-Checked: It feels right.

Obtainable: You can accomplish it in a reasonable amount of time with reasonable effort.

Actionable: You can take steps to making it happen right now.

Life-Oriented: It fits with your lifestyle right now. You have the support to make it happen.

Small Steps: The goal can be broken down into multiple, tiny steps.

Secret #12
Cross It Off the Bucket List

How Fun, Cool Stuff Can De-Stress Your Life

"We don't stop playing because we turn old,
but turn old because we stop playing." —Unknown

Resources:
Get downloadable worksheets and
tutorials for Secret #12
Fun, Cool Stuff at:

HHESecrets.com

*Use your smartphone to scan the below
QR code to go there now.*

Benefits:
- You will have more fun in life.
- Happiness level will increase.
- Stress will decrease.
- You will create happy memories.
- You will be a role model for your kids.
- You will become more comfortable with change.
- You will deal with challenges more effectively.

What's on Tap?

When was the last time you did something crazy and adventurous? I'm not talking about that time you took a new route home from work or you ordered a new kind of pizza. I'm talking about real, honest-to-goodness adventure that stretched you out of your comfort zone, got you thinking differently, and got you smiling.

I remember the very first moment I realized how important it was to get out of my comfort zone. I was in Hawaii by myself just three months after my husband had died. I thought a solo trip was just what I needed to relax, find a little peace, and start to heal. Boy was I wrong. I had somehow idiotically chosen the world's most romantic travel destination for this experimental trip and was being bombarded by scenes of love and togetherness at every turn. I was constantly on the verge of tears. But one night, I decided I needed to be brave. I needed to get over my fear and anxiety of seeing all that living and loving and just do my own living. I had avoided the dining room. I hadn't wanted to be the solo diner amongst all the candlelit tables, but I decided then and there that I could never grow or heal if I couldn't even sit in a room and eat amidst couples. So I threw on a cute sundress, put on a little makeup, grabbed a book to keep my company, and headed down to the restaurant to eat with all the love-struck tourists sharing the resort with me. At first I was totally uncomfortable. I felt like everyone was staring me down and wondering why I was such a loser for eating alone. But after a few minutes, I realized that no one cared. They were all absorbed in their own conversations and gazing into each other's eyes. I wasn't their focus. I had to be my own focus now. So I ordered a fancy meal and some wine and just relaxed for an hour. From that moment on, I felt just a tiny bit better every time I did something like that. Every time I would stretch and flex my courage muscles, my heart would break a little less and my stress would subside a little more, and I eventually started to look forward to my adventures.

In looking back, I know that those experiences that got me out of my routine were a huge part of what saved me from my own grief and stress. I built up resilience and confidence, and in the end, it has made me a stronger person who is much more resilient to stress, challenge, and change. But how can we get started on the path to adventure when we're so busy? And how can we overcome our fears to try new things? The Happy Hour Effect Secret #12 will reveal several of the secrets I discovered along the way that I teach to others as they seek out new adventures in their lives. We will learn:

- What fun, cool stuff is
- Why it is so important to have adventures
- Ideas to do your own fun, cool stuff
- Kid-friendly adventures
- Next steps

If you're ready to build in time for fun, cool stuff, this chapter is for you. And by being proactive in your life, you will reduce stress too!

What Is Fun, Cool Stuff?

We all do good stuff every day. It might be raising kids, working for a great company, or cooking a fabulous dinner. And yes, these things can be called fun and cool sometimes, but that isn't the kind of fun, cool stuff I'm talking about. I want you to think big here. Get out of your normal way of thinking. Think back to the times you've seen news stories about people who have done something a little bit crazy. I bet at least once you've said to yourself, "Wow, that's amazing, but I could never do that." That is the kind of fun, cool stuff I want you to embrace—those things that you think you could never do or that you're too scared to do.

One of my first attempts at doing something fun and cool (and completely outside of my comfort zone) was going to surf camp. Six months after my husband died, a friend asked me to go to Costa Rica to learn to surf. As a total klutz, this seemed like a bad idea. Plus, even though I didn't admit it back then, I was terrified to try something

Open Your Mind Through Travel

by Lee Abbamonte, world traveler

Travel can be the most therapeutic remedy in the world. Travel can take you away from the stress and grind of your daily life and take you into a stress-free environment far, far away. The feeling of freedom and relaxation can clear your mind and soul of your worries and concerns. To travel, whether it be a resort or adventure destination, can help you relieve stress, free your mind, and live longer and happier. Travel, in all its forms, can simply be an escape—a break from reality that is vital to your happiness and all-around health. Much like what exercise does for your body, travel can do for your mind, body, and soul.

- Travel opens your eyes and your mind to a whole new world.
- Travel is the best education you can receive.
- Travel brings you to places you've only dreamed about seeing.
- Travel makes adventures happen every day.
- Travel makes dreams come true.
- Travel gives you a sense of enormous accomplishment.
- Travel gives you something to look forward to.
- Travel is a lifetime journey that is never the same twice.
- Travel teaches you to become a traveler and not just a tourist.
- Travel humbles you and puts things into perspective.
- Travel shows you what poor really is.
- Travel shows you people overcoming the longest odds to live their life to the fullest.
- Travel shows you triumphs of the human spirit.
- Travel teaches you how to say *cheers* in thirty different languages.
- Travel teaches you to try new things.
- Travel makes you yearn to do new things.

Lee Abbamonte is a travel writer, travel expert, and the youngest American to visit every country in the world. Visit his official site at leeabbamonte.com.

new that might embarrass me or even kill me, leaving my daughter without both parents. But after weeks of back and forth with my own inner voices, I went. That trip was the turning point for the rest of my life! What if I hadn't gone on that trip? What if the cowardly lion inside of me had won and I had stayed home wallowing on the couch feeling sorry for myself? Would I have experienced in some other way the eye-opening a-ha moments that I had in Costa Rica that prompted me to make changes in my life? Maybe. But I'm certain I wouldn't feel as fulfilled or proud of myself as I felt after surviving five days of being pummeled in the ocean. I survived! And I grew and changed and became a braver and more resilient person. Now that's some fun, cool stuff!

In our daily lives, we can embrace this type of experience too. It may not be a trip to surf camp, but opportunities for adventure arise all the time. Maybe it's being asked to join a networking group, but you're scared to put yourself out there because you're an introvert. (Check—this one is very real for me.) Maybe you are asked on a date by someone who isn't your normal type. (Also totally relevant for me.) Or maybe a big, bold, life-changing opportunity comes along, like a new job, cross-country move, or travel destination. Whatever it is, these kinds of cool opportunities come along for a reason. They are tests. They are exercises that strengthen us—*if* we take advantage of them. If we don't, we may always feel regret and wonder "what if."

Lingering regret over missed opportunities can lead to stress because the emotions behind them keep rearing their ugly heads and disrupting our positive forward momentum. I still wonder if I should have accepted a job I was offered seven years ago! Even though I don't regret not having taken it—because I've found my true calling as a wellness and stress management guru and writer—I still wonder if I should have followed that opportunity at the time. Before my husband died, we had been contemplating a trip to New York City for the US Open tennis tournament. We ended up deciding to wait until the following year. But he died a week after the tournament ended. We would never get to take that trip. That "unfollowed choice" and a whole host of others still haunt me sometimes and remind me that I *must* take advantage of every opportunity that comes along.

Work, kids, relationships, money, hobbies—life is a patchwork of responsibilities and activities that fill our time. And doesn't it seem that our to-do lists expand to fill up every available second we have? Pretty soon, every day is a routine of carpools, job tasks, chores, and a few hours of sleep (if you're lucky). We get so sucked into the chaos and stress of everyday life that we forget to really live. But if we can build in time to explore our world in a deeper way, we will be happier, more fulfilled, and less stressed too.

Why Fun, Cool Stuff Is Good

There are so many ways to embrace the fun in life. Unfortunately, many of us feel like we don't have time for it, or we even feel guilty if we take time out for a little fun. But if you can build in time to do fun, cool stuff every single day, or even every week, you will benefit in so many ways. Here's how:

- Having fun prompts the release of feel-good chemicals by our brain. These feel-good chemicals do the obvious: make us feel good! Why wouldn't you want to be happier in your life?

- The feel-good chemicals released when we have fun counter-act stress chemicals. Why not replace feeling bad with feeling good? Win-win! Happy, fun, cool experiences naturally reduce stress.

- Fun is for everyone. Just because you are a responsible parent with a job and bills to pay doesn't mean it has to be all business all the time. Let your hair down and enjoy life sometimes. Have a good laugh. Have that extra drink (responsibly, of course). Do something crazy. If you're a Type A or uptight person (that used to be me in a big way), it will feel so good to let your expectations of yourself go and just indulge in fun for a while.

- Kids need to see that fun is good. Children play and indulge in creative pursuits, but as they age, the sense of fun slowly dissipates. But if we can keep a sense of adventure in their lives and in our own, we will be great role models for them.

- Fun, cool stuff creates fun, cool memories. When you look back on your life, it is often the unique, cool experiences that jump out as the most memorable. It's fun to have stories to tell your kids and grandkids. And you will feel a sense of pride and fulfillment from a life well lived.

- Fun, cool stuff pushes you out of your comfort zone. When this happens, you learn about who you are and what you can handle. You become more resilient to change and grow as a person.

- Bravery prompts more bravery. Once you've done one crazy, adventurous thing, you will have more confidence to keep trying new things. You've proven to yourself you can survive once, and you can do it again.

- Fun, cool stuff provides perspective. When you experience new things, it forces you to look at the world in a new way. This can help you work through problems more effectively and make choices that are based on experience.

I can't reinforce enough how important this chapter is. When we go after big dreams or partake in adventures in life, we are creating positive energy and positive forward momentum. That self-induced success is a natural stress killer because our sense of accomplishment wipes out the sense of failure that stress can cause. So get out there and have an adventure!

Take the Stress Out of Travel and Enjoy Your Next Getaway

by Casey Wohl, The Getaway Girl®

Sometimes just thinking about your next vacation is stressful—where to go, when to book, taking care of things at home before you leave…. Almost makes you want to nix the entire vacation. Whether your next excursion is a weekend away or a two-week retreat, studies show that getting away helps reduce stress levels and provides you with downtime to refocus and reenergize. So what are some ways you can avoid stressing out before and during your next trip?

1. **Embrace the uncertainty.** Unplanned things will happen to you while you travel, so it is best to embrace the uncertainty versus worry about it. You cannot control if your flight will be delayed, if you will get stuck in traffic, if your luggage will be lost, or if you will end up forgetting something. Allowing your mind to be open to uncertainty can actually help you cope. Plus, sometimes the uncertainty can make things fun… if you let it.

2. **Plan ahead.** The best places always book quickly, so make as many reservations in advance as you can for hotels, restaurants, spas, show tickets, cultural attractions, and other activities. The more reservations you can make ahead of time, the more organized your trip will be.

3. **Pack smartly.** You can save yourself a lot of stress by packing appropriately. Check the weather forecast and make a list of all the things you may need to bring with you. Pack

at least a day before you leave to avoid the stress of being rushed. Packing items that layer is always best, and (for ladies especially) stay within the same color scheme to lessen the amount of items you pack. Keep things you may need while traveling in your carry-on bag, but pack the rest of your items in your checked luggage to reduce your chances of getting held up at security points.

4. **Dress for comfort.** While people used to dress up for travel, we now know how important it is to dress for comfort when on the go. Be sure you wear (or bring) comfortable shoes. Also, be sure to pack clothes that you can comfortably move in and don't mind wearing all day. Plan to accessorize in order to dress up an outfit for easy day-to-night fashion modifications.

5. **Take care of your body.** Get plenty of sleep before and during your trip, take vitamins, and have some stress relievers on hand to decrease your chances of getting sick from the stress of travel and the germs recirculated in the airplane. Eat small meals throughout the day versus only a few large ones, and drink plenty of water to stay hydrated. Remember to stretch your legs frequently to keep circulation active.

Casey Wohl, known as The Getaway Girl®, is the author of the *Girls Getaway Guide* travel book series and is also the travel correspondent for Heartbeat Radio for Women and the nationally syndicated TV show *Daytime*. Discover more at GirlsGetawayGuide.net.

Adventure Ideas

Fun, cool stuff doesn't have to cost an arm and a leg or take a lot of time. You can create fun on a shoestring in your own backyard or experience luxurious, customized adventures in the furthest corners of the world. If you have things you have always wanted to do, start doing them. If you aren't sure where to start, here are some ideas to fit any budget to get you on the right path to fun, cool adventures that will enrich your life and reduce your stress in the process:

- Backyard, park, or beach picnics.
- Treasure hunts in the house, backyard, at museums, or at the park.
- Snow adventures: build snow people, forts, mazes; have snowball fights; create snow art right in the yard with paint and glitter; skiing, sledding, or skating.
- Slumber parties with kids, friends, a significant other: sleeping bags, popcorn, movies, makeovers, dance parties, etc.
- Disney World: In order to make the monetary investment worth it, please do yourself a favor and wait until your kids are old enough to really appreciate the experience and survive the long lines. Strollers are no fun here, so wait until your kids are old enough to walk the park. My daughter and I went after she turned five, and she was the perfect age to appreciate it, enjoy it, and remember it. And it will be a great memory for me too, instead of a frustrating memory of a long day with a crabby kid I had to carry and console all day.
- Beach vacations: Don't just lie in a hammock all day. Explore the shore. Look for shells. Take a boat trip. Go fishing. Snorkel or dive. Sightsee. Really immerse yourself in the culture and location.
- Service trips: Explore all the options out there to help others while getting out of the box. From building homes to teaching at schools to farming to research, there are countless opportunities to have an adventure *and* help make the world a better

place at the same time.

- Write a book: You can do this on your own or with your kids or spouse. It will be a unique and fun experience to bond and create memories.
- Cook together and make it fun.
- Attend community celebrations.
- Pick your own fruits and veggies.
- Better yet, grow your own fruits and veggies.
- Get a pet (or two) for fun, learning responsibility, and developing unconditional love with another living being.
- Attend live sporting events to feel the excitement and live the action.
- Learn a new skill, like knitting, surfing, juggling, line dancing, or anything else you've always wanted to learn but haven't.
- Go camping or hiking to experience nature firsthand.
- Spend time doing new things with family and friends.
- Eat outside.
- Do anything you have always wanted to do but haven't had the time or have been too scared to try!

This list could literally go on for an entire book. Don't limit your thinking to obvious things. Get online, read articles, think broadly, be bold. There are opportunities for adventure around every corner if you just open your eyes to see them and then have the courage to embrace them.

Now What?

When it comes to building in time for fun, cool stuff, most people don't make it a priority, and they fall back into their routines. The most important thing in making progress toward embracing opportunities is to make time for it. Block time on your calendar for fifteen minutes of web surfing for your next travel adventure. Read the events and travel sections of the newspaper and research things that sound interesting. Every week create an adventure for your kids and get motivated to continue when you see their reaction and that sparkle in their eyes (and yours). If you can make time for fun, cool stuff in your life, you will feel happier and more fulfilled, which inevitably leads to less stress. Here is a quick timeline of fun, cool ideas you can implement, starting today:

Secret #12 FUN STUFF Action Grid				
Action Step	Guidelines	Time to Implement	Simple/ Medium/ Hard	Fun/ Easy/ Important
Be Open to Adventure	Don't get so sucked into the chaos of everyday life that you forget to really live. Be open to the idea of adventures and doing fun, cool stuff.	1 day	S	FEI
Fun Is for Everyone	Just because you're a responsible adult with bills to pay or kids to raise doesn't mean you can't let your hair down and have some fun. Get back in touch with your inner child and just let go of your roadblocks. Have fun!	1 day	S	FEI
Dive In and Do It	Just go for it. Don't let the little voices in your head or other people talk you out of trying new things.	1 day	M	FI
Kids Need Fun	Kids need time to play and be kids. Show them how and give them the time to do it.	7 days	S	FEI
Be Brave	Rarely are we put into such dangerous situations that our lives are at risk. When it's time to try something new, just give it a shot. You may be surprised by the outcome.	14 days	H	FI
Get Perspective	Every activity has the opportunity for fun. A normal trip to the grocery store can become a treasure hunt. A family holiday can become a memorable tradition. Think differently and try new things.	14 days	M	FI
Stretch Limits	If you don't think you can do something, think again. Instead of bungee jumping, could you do indoor rock climbing? Instead of going on an African safari, could you have a wildlife spotting contest at a local park? Think differently and get out there.	21 days	H	FI
Create Memories	Doing fun, cool stuff will create positive memories for you and your loved ones. Start today!	30 days	S	FEI

Putting It All Together

Now that you've gone through the twelve secrets, it's time to start experimenting. Choose one or two of the ideas from the book that meet the GOALS criteria and feel like they will make the most impact in your life and bring you the most joy. Remember at the beginning of the book when I outlined GOALS? I hope you used them throughout the book as you decided which ideas to try first. If you need a little refresher, GOALS are:

- **Gut-Checked:** The goal "feels" right. You know in your gut that it is the right thing to do, and it energizes you. Fear may still be there, but the potential for success if you reach the GOAL overrides that fear.

- **Obtainable:** The goal isn't so lofty that you can never achieve it. It is something you can reach in a reasonable amount of time with reasonable amounts of effort.

- **Actionable:** The goal is able to be reached by solid, tangible actions you can take in your life. It isn't so complicated that you can't put simple action steps into a plan to reach it.

- **Life-Oriented:** The goal meshes with your day-to-day life. It fits into your family dynamic, your current reality, and your future dreams. It is a goal that is easily implemented into your schedule.

- Small Steps: The goal can be broken down into multiple mini tasks that are easy and fast to accomplish.

First, decide if an idea feels right in your gut. Then, be sure you can actually reach the goal. Next, be sure action can be taken on the idea right now. Finally, be sure the idea currently fits your lifestyle and needs. Start to break the idea down into mini GOALS—baby steps that can be taken to achieve the end result. For example, I gave the example of starting a scrapbooking business and beginning by doing research on the industry, attending events, reviewing finances, getting experience in the industry, and brainstorming ideas for your business. Use this example for your own GOALS and come up with an easy, step-by-step, actionable list of items you can start working on today.

Now it's time to give yourself the drive you need to make the changes a reality. First, put a timeframe in place to help motivate you to make progress. This is very, very important. Putting deadlines on your GOALS gives you a sense of urgency and makes it a real, living, achievable dream in process. Next, publicize your mini GOALS and timelines in some way. Putting your plans out there for the world to see holds you accountable so you don't just toss your file into the back of a drawer, never to be seen again. Start a blog, post it on Facebook or Twitter, or simply just start talking about it with others. They will be intrigued and continue to ask for updates. This support and encouragement will keep you moving forward to each new step.

Every couple of days, sit down and review your progress and make sure you are still on track. And most importantly, enjoy the process! Making changes is scary, but it's exciting too. Take pleasure in doing something for yourself. Take pride in the hard work you're putting in to achieve something big. And don't be afraid to talk about it. You can inspire others by your actions. Be a role model and soon your stress-less GOALS will become a reality!

As you go down this road to less stress, more happiness, and better health, I urge you to share your success with others. The more we can perpetuate the Happy Hour Effect lifestyle to the world, the more people there will be who can enjoy a more fulfilling life. The more people who get on board with the Stress Less Revolution, the more we can change the world in a positive way, simply by helping others experience the impact of minimizing stress to maximize life. Enjoy your journey through this crazy thing called life, and cheers to a less stressed you!

Set Goals, Stress Less

by Randy Ganther, success expert and entrepreneur

In the most simple terms, goal setting reduces stress because it allows us to know where we are going and what is likely to happen to us on the way. Most of our stress comes from the unknown, and over 97 percent of our fears and worries never happen. Therefore, we are creating an overwhelming amount of unneeded stress.

Setting goals eliminates the majority of your stress because you don't have to worry where you are going to end up on a daily, weekly, or yearly basis. If you walked into the cabin of an airplane and told the pilot, "Just take me anywhere," you'd wonder and worry the entire time about what is going to happen along the way. If you know where you are going, you don't have to worry about the little things in-between point A and point B. You know that's just part of the journey, and since you are focused on where you will be, the small issues along the way are simply minor inconveniences that are an expected part of the journey and not something to stress over.

When you have goals, you know what you need to accomplish the following day to get to where you are going, so I like to set out my schedule at night, with my list of things I need to accomplish—in order. This lets me sleep well, knowing my next day will start off correctly; I don't have to fill my mind with clutter as I lie in bed, which allows me to doze off faster and deeper, waking with a sense of control and direction.

Randy Ganther is a peak-performance speaker and author and the creator of the book series *The Little Book for Huge Success*™ as well as his *Maximum Success*™ series of books. For more than thirty years Randy has been studying and interviewing successful men and women in all walks of life. Randy has excelled in the world of sports, as diverse as winning state- and regional-level powerlifting championships and even a World Horseshoe Championship. Randy's system for peak performance is contained in his books and programs. Learn more at RandyGanther.com.

How to Master the Art of Happiness with Goal Setting

by Heidi DeCoux, organizational and productivity expert

Many of us have so many things to do and handle each day that we feel overwhelmed! And the process of feeling happy instead starts with prioritizing and defining what's important to you.

We address that issue in my *Power & Accomplishment* time-mastery program. In the program, we take the first step to happiness by creating three main goals, or identifying three main priorities, in each area of your life. The areas of your life may include: health, family, spirituality, career, community, recreation, hobbies, etc. You can do this *now* and get a taste of the program.

- Write down three main goals or priorities in each area.
- Post your goals and priorities somewhere where you will look at them often.

- Before adding anything to your to-do list, and before taking on new opportunities, look at your goals and priorities.
- Ask yourself,
  - o Is this task or opportunity in alignment with my priorities?
  - o Will it move me closer to my goals?
- If the answer is *no*, then don't add the item to your to-do list or take on the new opportunity.

When you are crystal clear on your priorities and goals, it's becomes very easy to say *no*, or at least *not yet*, to new opportunities.

The next step in the art of prioritizing is to rank your to-do list by impact on your life. The highest rank goes to the action that will move you toward your goals the fastest.

It's easy to get bogged down in minutia. By definition, minutia makes very little impact on our lives. Identify minutia, then eliminate it or delegate it! Focus on the big-impact actions!

Heidi DeCoux is an organizing and productivity expert and founder of ClearSimpleLiving.com. You can get free access to on-demand workshops, checklists, and a home organization e-kit now at ClearSimpleLiving.com.

Acknowledgments

A heartfelt thank you to all of the friends, colleagues, fans, and supporters who have helped make Happy Hour Effect a real and powerful force in people's lives. Thanks to my agent, Jill Kramer at Waterside Productions, for your belief in this project. Thanks to my editor, David Michael Gettis at Goodman Beck Publishing, for reading through all my drivel and fixing all my mistakes—and for taking so much time out of his own life to work on this book. Thanks to Goodman Beck Publishing for taking a chance on *The Happy Hour Effect* and for your mission of helping others live better lives. We are in agreement! Thanks to my publicists, Sara Lien and Annie Scranton, for helping me get my message out to the world, and to my blog tour manager, Emily Hedges, for rockin' the blogosphere with my words. Thanks to my furry mutt, Cosmo, for keeping me company during this lonely task of writing a book. RIP, buddy! And most importantly, thanks to my family—my parents, siblings, in-laws, and my daughter—for putting up with my crazy ideas and supporting me through all of them. I love you all!

Resources

Chapter Materials:
Every Secret in this book has corresponding worksheets, videos, and other fun resources to help you reach your goals. Simply scan the QR code within each chapter to go right to the good stuff. Access all of the materials at HHESecrets.com.

Website:
Be sure to check out all of our classes, training materials, health supplements, and more at HappyHourEffect.com.

Social Media:
And don't forget to follow us on Twitter, Facebook, and Pinterest by searching *Happy Hour Effect*. You will get free stress-less tips, articles, and inspiration to live healthier and happier every single day.

Speaking:
Need a speaker? Kristen is a renowned stress expert, speaker, and seminar leader. She provides corporate wellness programs, keynote presentations, breakout sessions, and custom programs for companies and organizations around the world. Contact her at: kristen@happyhoureffect.com

About the Author

Kristen K. Brown, *The Queen of Stress Relief*, is a coach, bestselling and award-winning author, webTV host, speaker, and the founder of Happy Hour Effect LLC and WidowMommy.com. She has her master's certificate in integral theory, is a certified holistic health coach, and is a fifteen-year corporate America veteran. Her debut memoir, *The Best Worst Thing*, was about her journey to a new life after the unexpected death of her husband from a heart attack at the age of thirty when their daughter was just an infant. *The Happy Hour Effect* is Kristen's highly anticipated second release.

Kristen has won the Royal Dragonfly Book Award, Readers' Favorite Book Award, SWIBA Award for Author of the Year, and has been nominated for two American Business Awards and two International Women in Business Awards. She has been featured on television, radio, print, and online, including CBS, Fox, NBC, ABC, Working Mother, CNN.com, and US Weekly.

Kristen enjoys gardening, meditation, cooking, yoga, travel, reading, and all things self-improvement focused. Kristen has traveled the world for both business and pleasure and enjoys learning about new cultures. She is a member of Women of Words, The Loft Literary Center, Film Independent, Femfessionals, and a volunteer for the American Heart Association. She lives in Minneapolis, Minnesota, with her five-year-old daughter, and she will do almost anything for bacon.